MICROECONOMICS

CASES AND SCENARIOS

Learn Economics via Cases and Scenarios

Elijah M. James, Ph. D.

Canadian Cataloguing in Publication Data

James, Elijah M.

Microeconomics Cases and Scenarios

ISBN 978-1-7383576-4-2

EJ Publishing

663 White Hills Run

Hammonds Plains

Nova Scotia, Canada B4B 1W7

Lovingly dedicated to the memory
of the late Robert Josiah who was
a sincere friend indeed.

TABLE OF CONTENTS

PREFACE

Brief Description

This book is designed to give students a more comprehensive grasp of economics. The advantages of the case method are well documented. The cases and scenarios that comprise this book place the student in *possible* economic situations where he or she learns not just economic jargon and theory but is also given opportunities to apply theory in providing solutions to possibly real economic problems. Economics comes to life in the various cases and scenarios provided, and very importantly, students perceive the importance of economics in their own lives, present and future. Every effort is made to ensure that the student is deeply involved with the material and that a high level of interest is maintained throughout.

Microeconomics: Cases and Scenarios is intended primarily for students taking courses in introduction to microeconomics, but students taking intermediate microeconomics will also find the book to be very useful. Though not intended as a stand-alone text, it is possible to use this book as the main text, supplemented by other relevant material.

Outstanding Features

The following are some of the outstanding features of *Microeconomics: Cases and Scenarios:*

- ♦ Highly interactive and student-centered
- ♦ A novel and effective use of cases and scenarios to learn economics

- ◆ Verbal skills, critical thinking skills, and analytical skills are developed
- ◆ The approach emphasizes the relevance of economics in students' lives
- ◆ Visual aids (graphs) are used extensively
- ◆ Designed to be used in any English-speaking country
- ◆ Unparalleled for help with test and exam preparation.

A concerted effort has been made to bring analysis to bear on real problems. All answers are purported to be written by the student reading the cases and scenarios through the performance of assigned tasks in a variety of situations. Thus, the student is fully integrated into the learning process.

Pedagogical Features

There is no shortage of pedagogical features in this book.

Tasks

At the end of each case or scenario, the student is asked to perform a specific task. The performance of that task helps the student to develop written communication, critical thinking, problem-solving, and analytical skills. At the same time, the student learns how to apply microeconomic theory to the design of microeconomic policy.

Pictures

Pictures are used extensively throughout the book to create the mood and to set the stage for the scenarios. Pictures are used in this book in much the same way as music is used in films. They create a relationship with the scenario, create the appropriate atmosphere, evoke desired emotions, and add a sense of reality to the cases and scenarios. They take the student from where he or she is to where he or she ought to be.

Humour

Humour is used liberally to capture and maintain the student's interest. Other pedagogical advantages of humour are: the enhancement of the learning environment and hence learning outcomes, a higher retention rate, and the reduction of anxiety, all of which are conducive to learning.

Sample Tests

An entire section of this book (Part 7) is devoted to sample tests. It includes six sample tests on the material typically covered in a course in introductory microeconomics. Answers are provided so that students can compare their answers with those given. These are pedagogical devices as well as grade boosters.

Other pedagogical tools

A wide variety of other pedagogical tools are used throughout the book. The cases and scenarios consist, for example, of dialogues, lectures, radio and TV shows, picnics, conversations, internet searches, study groups, conventions, travel, games, and, believe it or not, even dreams.

Level

The book is intended for undergraduate students taking courses in introductory microeconomics. The book does not assume any prior knowledge of the subject on the part of the student. Students taking intermediate microeconomics will also find the book of immense value.

The Competition

Although the idea of using cases and scenarios in economics is not new, the nature of the cases and scenarios and the manner in which they are used in this book are unique. In my research, I have not been able to find a book that is similar to *Microeconomics: Cases and Scenarios*. I am not aware of any similar works completed or in progress. In general, the book will compete in the market with other learning guides and alternative formats, but I know of no close substitutes for *Microeconomics: Cases and Scenarios*.

Acknowledgements

My indebtedness to friends, colleagues, teachers, and students seems to multiply with every book I write. When I decided to write this book, I discussed the idea with several people, all of whom gave their enthusiastic endorsements.

I am extremely grateful to many of my students at Dawson College who willingly agreed to use some of the scenarios. Their comments served to improve the effectiveness of the book significantly.

It would be remiss of me if I did not single out my friend and colleague Dr. Alaka Ganguli, who strongly encouraged the use of cases and scenarios in the teaching of economics. Thank you, Alaka, you have been an inspiration. Dr. Worku Aberra of Dawson College has been an ardent supporter through the years. Thank you, Worku, I can never repay you.

Finally, to my dear Sister, Vera, thank you for your unflinching support of my work all through the years. Your example of discipline was followed throughout the process of writing this book.

I thank you all.

Elijah James

PART I

INTRODUCTION

You are employed as a Human Resources Officer at the Large Variety Corporation (LVC)—a fictitious company that produces and sells a large variety of household items such as electric fans, kitchen utensils, clocks, reading lamps, vacuum cleaners, etc. At its last board meeting, the company discussed the possibility of hiring an economist. Knowing that you have studied economics, the Human Resources Manager has asked you to prepare a document detailing why it would be a good idea to hire an economist for her to include in her presentation at the next board meeting.

Task

Your task is to prepare a 250-word report for the Human Resources Manager explaining convincingly why it would be advantageous for LVC to hire an economist.

Scenario 2: What Exactly do Economists do?

At a meeting of the Board of Directors of the NOW Corporation, there was a lively discussion regarding employing an economist. After listening to various arguments, the Board decided to employ the services of an economist on a full-time basis because its main competitors have hired economists and they seem to be prospering as a result. The Human Resources Manager has to prepare a job description for the economist's position and has called upon you to draft such a job description.

Task

You are required to draft the job description so that the Human Resources Department can post the job. Your description must show that you know what economists do.

Scenario 3: Economic Growth—A Controversial Issue? Applying Economic Reasoning

At a city hall meeting in Econoville (an imaginary city), there is a heated debate about the effects of economic growth. One group extols the virtues of economic growth while the other denounces the evils of more economic growth. The outcome of this debate is crucial for the decision that the city has to make regarding its tangible support (or lack of it) for more economic growth.

The supporters of more economic growth claim that had it not been for economic growth, the standard of living in Econoville would not be anywhere close to where it is now. Economic growth must be credited with educational opportunities now easily available, with a health care system that is the envy of many, and with Econoville's ability to provide the high level of services offered to its residents—excellent garbage collection, well-paved and properly maintained streets, numerous parks, adequate housing, etc. They maintain that the pursuit of economic growth is mandatory if Econoville is to be able to maintain or improve the well-being of its residents.

The detractors of more economic growth emphasize the view that although economic growth enables residents to purchase bigger and more beautiful homes, buy bigger and more luxurious cars, take more vacations to exotic places, and enjoy all the amenities that that Econoville is able to provide, these are only *physical things* and they do not guarantee happiness. Moreover, they claim, economic growth comes at the expense of more traffic congestion, greater environmental degradation, and increased emotional stress that take a toll on our health and wellness. They maintain that more economic growth is not worth the cost.

Task

Your task is to apply the economic way of thinking to this controversial issue so that the city can make an informed choice.

Scenario 4: Economics, a Science? Never!

Imagine that you have come across the following article in a magazine:

The great advances that have been made in science have inspired such confidence in anything scientific that many disciplines are finding ways to classify themselves as sciences. It is well known that fields of study such as physics, chemistry, biology, and botany are sciences. In such fields of study, observation, measurement, and experimentation in laboratories are what make them science. I heard someone talking about *economic science* the other day and I could hardly believe my ears. The speaker was trying to make the point that economics was a science. I said to myself: "What! Economics a science? It can never be." Economists do nothing but philosophize on certain aspects of the economy.

If economics can claim to be a science then dog catchers are scientists.

Nilton Freeman

Task

As a student of economics, you are to write a letter to Mr. Freeman, defending the right of economics to be considered a science.

Scenario 5: Why don't they listen? Economists as Advisers

The ruling party of a particular country hired two economic advisers at very attractive salaries to advise the prime minister on economic matters. The role of the economic advisers is stated specifically as follows: "To study the impact of government policies on the economy and to advise the Prime Minister accordingly." Six months after the employment of the economic advisers, one of them was heard saying: "I am so frustrated in this job. We have done an excellent job of analyzing the effects of government policies, and the Prime Minister has openly expressed his total satisfaction with our work. Yet he has not followed our advice." Why don't these leaders listen to the advice of their advisers?"

Task

Your task is to answer the question posed in this scenario. Why don't they listen?

The members of the Department of Economics at Athelma University (fictitious) went on a picnic. As might be expected, they started to debate different aspects of the economy. The discussion began with Dan asking Paul whether he had come to accept the wisdom of imposing a tax on cigarettes. Paul responded that he remained firm in his position that the tax was just another example of a tax grab to stuff the government's coffers. Paul then asked Jim, who was sitting opposite him at the picnic table, if he was still adamant that the reduction in the rate of interest would have only minimal impact on the level of investment. Jim responded that he was at a loss trying to figure out why Paul insisted that the impact on investment would be huge. Betty, Dan's wife, then interrupted with the suggestion that they ate lunch.

Task

Your task is to study the discussion in the scenario and explain why these economists disagreed.

The following dialogue took place between Miss Green and Mr. Brown on the subject of scarce resources in Jorobel (an imaginary country).

Miss Green: All this talk about scarce resources in Jorobel is getting to me.

Mr. Brown: It's utterly ridiculous. We have an abundance of all kinds of resources in Jorobel.

Miss Green: For sure. We have lots of land, a relatively large and growing population, an abundance of water in the form of rivers and lakes, and deposits of precious metals with which no country can compare.

Mr. Brown: You see; they take this idea of scarcity and try to apply it everywhere. Well, it certainly does not apply to us in Jorobel. Ours is a land flowing with milk and honey. No scarcity here. See you at the party later.

Miss Green: Yes, I'll be there.

Task

Answer the following questions based on the dialogue between Miss Green and Mr. Brown.

a. What concept of scarcity might Miss Green and Mr. Brown have in mind when they denied the existence of scarcity in Jorobel?

b. Is there scarcity in Jorobel? How so?

Scenario 8: The Cost of Attending University May be More than You Think

John has recently graduated from university with a degree in economics and is currently employed full-time as a junior economist with Zest Sales (a fictitious marketing company) at an annual salary of $40,000. Prior to attending university, John worked as a sales representative at a salary of $30,000. While attending university, he had to live away from home. The following information about the annual cost of attending university is available:

Tuition	$12,000
Other fees	2,500
Room	6,500
Meals	5,500
Books	1,400
Insurance	1,000
Miscellaneous	600
Total	$29,500

Task

Answer the following questions based on the scenario given:

a) What important cost item is missing from the calculation of John's total cost of attending university?

b) Calculate John's total cost of attending university.

c) If John was unemployed before he decided to attend university because he just could not find a job, what then would be his total cost of attending university?

Scenario 9: Enrolment Planning at a University. Anything to do with Opportunity Cost?

Best Business University (BBU) – an imaginary private university—is well known for the high quality of its business courses. BBU is not unlike the university shown here.

An administrator from BBU met with the university's economic consultant to discuss plans for enrolment for the next three years. The forecasted unemployment figures for the next five years for the region from which the university draws the vast majority of its students are presented below.

Year	Unemployment rate
1st year	10%
2nd year	15%
3rd year	21%
4th year	16%
5th year	15%

The following conversation is what occurred between the university administrator and the economic consultant:

Admin: Here we are again, planning for enrolment.

Con: Yes. I can't believe it's an entire year since we met. Time really flies.

Admin: We should have an easy time now though. With the employment situation for the next few years, it is clear that our enrolment will fall significantly. It will be difficult for people to pay school fees. We should shelve the plan to add additional classrooms.

Con: I don't see it that way. I think we should expect an increase in enrolment since more students will be seeking admission. We should actually plan to add additional classrooms.

Admin: What? That is strange…..

Task

Your task is to write a report of about 180 words explaining whose view of the course of enrolment at BBU is correct.

Scenario 10: Calculating Real Profit. The Economist's Approach

Your aunt, Violet, after working at the Bread of Life Bakery and Café (a fictitious business) for seven years, was promoted to Assistant Manager. The owner of the bakery decided to sell the store. It was Violet's dream to own her own bakery, so this, she thought, was a golden opportunity. She bought Bread of Life. It was just a month earlier that she turned down an offer of $60,000 a year to manage a competing bakery.

Violet has often wondered whether or not she had made the right decision by refusing the offer to manage the competing bakery. The income statement for the first year of operation after Violet bought the store is as follows:

Sales	$1,500,000
Direct cost of goods sold	900,000
Gross margin	**600,000**
Operating expense:	
Advertising and promotion	8,000
Payroll expense	170,000
Interest and taxes	120,000
Permits and licenses	500
Miscellaneous	11,000
Total operating expenses	**309,500**
Net profit	**290,500**

Wanting to put as much money as possible back into the business, Violet did not draw a salary for the entire year. She looked at the bottom line and smiled. She had made almost $300,000.

Task

Your task is to review the information provided in the scenario from an economic perspective and prepare a 160-180 word statement so that Violet can know how well Bread of Life has done in its first year of operation.

Scenario 11: Presentation for the Park. Explain it with Production-Possibility Curves

The city of Parkland (a fictitious city) has a fixed amount of money (budget) to spend on its recreation parks. A decision is being made as to whether to use the funds to create additional parking spaces or to increase the number of playground equipment. Not surprisingly, people who drive to the parks support the idea of additional parking places while pedestrians tend to support the idea of more playground equipment.

The Director of Parks and Recreation for the city is preparing a presentation for an upcoming town hall meeting. The objective of the presentation is to present different scenarios and explain the possibilities that each scenario offers. In his presentation, he wants to use a set of graphs because he believes that the visual aids will add effectiveness to his presentation. The following are the main points that he wants to illustrate graphically.

a) With its given budget, the city cannot provide more parking spaces *and* more playground equipment at the same time.
b) The city allocates additional funds to the Department of Parks and Recreation with the condition that such funds can be used only to expand the parking areas.
c) Because of a significant increase in the number of families moving to Parkland, the demand for parking spaces increases.
d) Parkland decides to increase the budget of the Department of Parks and Recreation.

Economic Consulting Associates (ECA), your employer, has been given a contract to produce the necessary graphs for the Director of Parks and Recreation.

Task

As a junior economic consultant with the company, you have been given the assignment to produce the series of graphs requested by the Director. Your task is to produce the graphs as requested, in a document containing between 180-200 words, and applying the appropriate economic model.

Assume that you were at a political rally organized by the Socialist Party. Speaker after speaker extolled the virtues of a command economy in which the main factors of production are owned and used by the government. Speaker 1 spoke about the inability of a capitalist system to automatically generate full employment. Speaker 2 spoke about the tendency for certain goods to be under-produced in a free-market economy, and speaker 3 spoke about the tendency for the environment to be overlooked in a capitalist economy. And on and on they went. A lone, high-pitched voice shouted: "Down with the free-market system." Not a drum was heard for capitalism, and not even a funeral note as the free enterprise system was buried at that rally.

Task

You are a staunch believer in the free market system. You are to prepare a statement of about 250 words in which you explain the main advantages of a market-oriented economic system.

Scenario 13: What is the Question? The Free Market Answers

(Cathy and Eugene are sitting in the cafeteria. They had just finished a class with Professor Query. The following conversation ensued).

Eugene: Professor Query sure asks lots of questions. Did you get that "what, how and for whom" thing that he was trying to explain?

Cathy: Yea. You didn't get it?

Eugene: Sort of, except for the part when he was talking about how a free enterprise economic system answers the "what" question.

Cathy: Do you understand the "what" question?

Eugene: Oh yes. That part is easy. But I don't understand how the free enterprise system answers the question; and we have to know it because Professor Query says it will be on the test.

Cathy: O.K. Let me explain it to you. It's really not that difficult.

Task

Your task is to play the role of Cathy and explain to Eugene how the free enterprise system answers the "what" question.

Scenario 14: Search and You will Find the Circular Flow Model

One evening, you and your best friend were searching for something on the Internet. After a long search, you finally found what you were looking for. Earlier, you were telling your friend who has never taken an economics course, about your economics class and how much you were enjoying it. That sparked her interest in economics so she suggested that you search for economics just to see what you would find. You agreed. A short time after you began your search, the following diagram popped up.

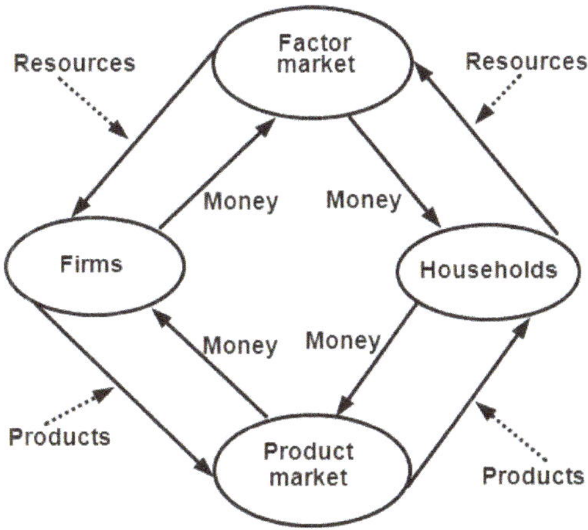

"What is that?" your friend inquired.

Task

Your task is to explain the diagram to your friend.

In a city with a population of about 550,000, there are many service stations selling gasoline. It has been observed for the past three years that the price of gasoline fluctuated considerably and quite frequently. Many claim that the fluctuations are due to price-fixing and collusion by the oil companies.

You are employed by a reputable economic consulting firm, Economic Consulting Associates (ECA) as a junior economist. In an attempt to dispel any idea of collusion, an executive of one of the major oil companies has contracted ECA to show that the fluctuations in the price of gasoline can be due to factors other than price-fixing and collusion.

Task

Your supervisor has assigned to you the task of preparing a 250-page document demonstrating that price fluctuations can be due to factors other than collusion. Specifically, she wants you to use the model of price determination with graphs in your report.

It has been some time since Best Business University (BBU) revised its residence pricing policy. The university has accommodation for 105 students in its dormitories and currently charges $2,500 per semester per student. The university's housing department is interested in knowing:

a) Whether the university's current residence pricing policy poses a problem.
b) What price change, if any, the university should make.
c) The appropriate rate per semester that the university should charge for accommodation in its dormitories.
d) The effect of an increase in the price of its accommodation on the demand for accommodation at its dormitories.
e) The possible impact on the demand for accommodation at the dormitories at BBU if accommodation at neighbouring residences becomes more expensive.

The university's housing manager is authorized to engage the services of your employer, Economic Consulting Associates (ECA) to analyze the market for housing accommodation at BBU.

The following data on the demand for accommodation at BBU are available.

Price per room /semester ($)	Quantity of rooms demanded /semester
2,800	100
2,700	105
2,600	110
2,500	115
2,400	120
2,300	125
2,200	130

Task

As a junior economist with ECA, you are given the assignment to analyze the market for accommodation at BBU and provide the information required by the housing department in a 150-175 word report.

Scenario 17: Arise and Shine: The Market for Coffee

Violet's Bread of Life Bakery has received a shipment of 2,000 packages of coffee. She intends to price them at $4 per package. A reputable economist has determined that the demand for coffee at Bread of Life is as follows:

Price per package ($)	Quantity demanded
4.50	500
4.00	1,000
3.50	1,500
3.00	2,000
2.50	2,500
2.00	3,000

Remembering your earlier work in reviewing her income statement, Violet has asked your opinion regarding her intention to price the coffee at $4 per package. Specifically, she wants to know:

a) If her intended price of $4 per package will enable her to sell her entire stock, leaving customers not wanting to buy more or less.

b) What price change, if any, she will have to make to enable her to accomplish her objective.

c) The impact of a change in the price of a similar package of coffee at Daily Bread, a competing bakery, on the demand for her product.

Task

You are required to analyze the market for coffee at Bread of Life Bakery and Café and provide the information requested by Violet in a 170-190 word report.

Scenario 18: The Politics and Economics of Minimum Wage Legislation

It's three weeks before the next election and, as usual, the politicians are scrambling for votes. One thing that can be counted on to win votes is the promise of an increase in the minimum wage. This is one of the main planks in the platform of the opposition party. Mr. David Smith (he thinks he is a descendant of Adam Smith), leader of the ruling party, mused: "Is there any way that I can mount an argument against that minimum wage idea? Oh, I know! I'll ask our economist. Economists usually have a different perspective on such things.

Task

Your task is to prepare an economic analysis of the effects of minimum wage legislation for Mr. Smith so that he can attack the plan of the opposition party.

The city of Pleasantville (a fictitious city) established a Rent Control Board to regulate the rent that landlords can charge their tenants. The objective is to help tenants by preventing rent from rising too fast. Before the institution of rent control, the mayor of Pleasantville used to boast of the beauty of his city with its well-maintained apartment buildings. Ten years after the establishment of the Rent Control Board, slums have begun to appear for the first time in Pleasantville.

Task

Your task is to answer the following questions.

a) Explain how rent control might have contributed to the development of slums in Pleasantville.

b) What alternative step might the city have taken to prevent rent from rising in Pleasantville?

Scenario 20: Farmers on the Move. Quotas and All That

A group of farmers complained that in spite of huge productivity increases in the farming sector over the years, farmers still earn relatively low incomes while the rest of society benefits from the low price of food. They decided to march to the office of the Minister of Agriculture to protest low farm incomes. Marchers carried placards bearing signs such as those shown here.

The Minister of Agriculture addressed the farmers, promising that he would immediately address their plight. Shortly thereafter, the government passed a law imposing a quota on the quantity of farm products that farmers can produce.

Task

You are to answer the following questions.

a) Why might farmers not have benefited from increases in their own productivity?
b) Explain how the quota might improve the well-being of farmers.

Scenario 21: Here Comes Professor Noce. Beware of False Demand and Supply Doctrines

Host: Good morning, listeners. Welcome to Radio 101. This morning we are privileged to have Professor Noce with us for the next 30 minutes. Good morning Professor. Welcome.

Professor: Thank you. It's good to be here. Good morning listeners.

Host: Professor, before we begin, I notice that your name, if read from right to left becomes econ, which is often an abbreviation for economics.

Professor: They joke about that all the time in the Economics Department, but it is just a coincidence.

Host: Professor Noce is an economics professor at Nosuch University of Noneconomic Science (NUNS) and he has agreed to answer some questions about economics. Professor, let me begin with this question. We have noticed that the demand for laptop computers has increased significantly over the years. Is this because of a fall in their prices over the years?

Professor: Definitely. There can be no doubt about it. Whenever the price of an item like a laptop computer falls, the demand will always increase. It's what we call the law of demand.

Host: Professor, what will happen to the price of an item when its demand increases?

Professor: Well, we are not sure. You see, when demand increases, the price rises, but when the price rises, the demand decreases which causes the price to fall, so we don't know whether the price will end up being higher or lower.

Host: Very interesting! Professor, a listener wants to know what complementary goods are.

Professor: Well, ahh… My students at Nosuch U often ask this question. Complementary goods are goods that make the user feel proud or gratified. For example, an expensive outfit that makes you feel really good when you wear it is a complementary good. All luxury items such as diamonds, yachts, Rolex watches, and Gucci leather bags are called complementary goods.

Host: People often talk about supply and demand simultaneously as if they are inseparable. How are they related?

Professor: That's a good question. I emphasize this relationship in my classes at NUNS. Whenever demand increases, supply will also increase; and whenever supply increases, demand will also increase. That shows how closely related they are.

Host: Thank you, Professor. You have certainly enlightened us. It's always a pleasure to have you on our show. I look forward to having you again.

Professor: Thank you very much. It was a pleasure.

Task

After studying Professor Noce's responses, you are to indicate any errors in his responses and correct them.

Scenario 22: Sally's Dilemma—Math to the Rescue

Your cousin, Sally, never saw the use for mathematics in high school and often claimed that it was just a waste of time. After graduating from high school, Sally spent two years in the Young Entrepreneur Program at college, after which, she opened Boutique Sally, a classy store in the City Mall. Sally has ordered 100 small bags and would like to know what price she should charge in order to just clear the market for her bags. She was told that the demand for her bags per month was given by the following equation:

$$Qd = 130 - 3P$$

What does that mean? Sally wondered. She was overheard saying that she wished she had paid more attention to mathematics in school.

Because of successful advertising, the demand for Sally's bags increased by 15 for the next month. Her monthly order has remained at 100 bags and again, she wants to price them so that she has neither a shortage nor a surplus.

Task

You are to use the information provided in this scenario to determine the price that Sally should charge for her bags so that she will have the relevant information.

PART 2

ELASTICITY AND CONSUMER CHOICE

Cathy and Angela just missed the bus after their microeconomics class, so they decided to take the 20-minute walk home. They thought it was a good opportunity for them to discuss the topic they were studying in class—elasticity of demand. Cathy began the discussion:

Cathy: Professor Norton was amazing this afternoon. She was really in her element.

Angela: I couldn't agree with you more. She really did justice to that topic. There is one thing I didn't understand though.

Cathy: What is that? Maybe I can help because I think I got it.

Angela: It's the part about raising and lowering price to raise revenue.

Cathy: Oh! That is really easy.

Angela: Not to me.

Cathy: Listen. It's as simple as this. Assume that you are selling something. If you increase the price, you make more money so your revenue increases. If you reduce your price, you make less money so your revenue falls. Understand now?

Angela: Sure. It's not so difficult after all. Thanks.

Cathy: You are welcome. No problem. See you tomorrow.

Angela: O.K. See you tomorrow.

The two friends separated, each going to her individual home.

Task

What is wrong (if anything) with Cathy's explanation?

Professor Noce is an economics professor at Nosuch University of Noneconomic Science (NUNS). Note that Noce, if read from right to left, becomes econ, which is often used as an abbreviation for economics. Below is the professor lecturing to one of his classes.

Professor Noce: In a previous lecture, we highlighted the close relationship between economics and mathematics. In many cases, the concepts are identical. A perfect example is elasticity and slope. In economics, we say elasticity; in mathematics, we say slope. We are referring to the same concept. If a mathematician draws a steep line, she will refer to it as having a high slope. An economist will refer to it as being inelastic. The two concepts are identical. It's a matter of semantics. Just remember, high slope is inelastic while low slope is elastic.

Task

Your task in this scenario is to identify the error in Professor Noce's argument and correct it.

Scenario 25: Either There is a Response or no Response to a Change in Price. Don't be Confused.

These people are so involved with their economics that they even take it with them to the beach. It was a beautiful Sunday, and the blue sky dotted with patches of white cloud and a gentle breeze blowing out of the east all conspire to make a beach picnic irresistible. John called his friend, Mark, and suggested that they go to the beach for a picnic.

It was a beautiful Sunday, and the blue sky dotted with patches of white cloud and a gentle breeze blowing out of the east all conspire to make a beach picnic irresistible. John called his friend, Mark, and suggested that they go to the beach for a picnic.

Mark: That's a fabulous idea. I was speaking with Isabel just a few minutes ago and she made the same suggestion. Let me check with her and get back to you.

John: Okay buddy.

(About an hour and a half later, John, Isabel, and Mark arrived at the beach. They found a picnic table that was just right for them. After a walk on the beautiful beach and the usual joking around, the three friends sat at the picnic table. One of the things they had in common was that they were taking the same economics class with the same professor. Mark began the discussion):

Mark: What do you guys think about that elasticity thing?

Isabel: What specifically do you mean?

Mark: I am referring to the idea that the coefficient of price elasticity of demand is negative.

John: Oh, that! I always thought that products such as elastic bands, rubber bands, and bra straps were elastic while products such as forks, cars, and iron were inelastic.

Isabel: Come on, John. Be serious. Everyone knows that it is not the products that are elastic or inelastic, but the *demand* for them.

Mark: If elasticity is a measure of the degree of responsiveness, then if there is no response, the elasticity should be zero. If there is some response, then the measure should be positive.

John: Mark, I think I can help you with that.

(Before John could offer his explanation, a thick cloud appeared overhead, and the three friends decided to head home).

Task

You are to assume that John had the correct explanation. What was he going to say?

After hearing about the land flowing with milk and honey, you decided to visit Jorobel. Upon your arrival, you were greeted by a friend who held a high position in the government and who informed you that the only economist in the country had recently resigned and had left the country. However, she had left a set of data in the form of tables. Your friend showed you the following table:

Table 1 Data for the Demand for Wallets in Jorobel

Price ($)	Quantity Bought (000)	Total Revenue ($000)	Elasticity Coefficient
10	100		
9	120		
8	140		
7	160		
6	180		
5	200		

Task

a) You are to complete Table 1 for the total revenue from wallets in Jorobel.
b) Compute the price elasticity of demand for each price change and complete the elasticity coefficient column.
c) Explain the relation that you observe between total revenue and price elasticity of demand.

Scenario 27: What items to tax?

It's a Wednesday morning and Jack and Jill are enjoying their 30-minute drive to work. Jill is talking to Jack about a project she is working on, and telling him how much she enjoys working at the Mode Corporation (fictitious). They come to a red light and while they are waiting for the light to change to green, Jack, who works for the Revenue Department, announces that he has to come up with a list of items to tax so that the government can earn some much-needed revenue.

Jill responds with the question: Why doesn't the government just levy taxes on the most expensive items? After all, people don't have a choice.

Task

Your task is to come up with a list of 10 items that the government can tax to raise revenue.

Scenario 28: The True Meaning of Utility

Sarah likes to express her thoughts verbally. Here are her thoughts on utility:

"One of the good things about studying economics is that it uses familiar terms to describe concepts. *Utility* is a case in point. The items pictured below are all very useful. Therefore, they have a high utility.

On the other hand, there are some items, like exercise equipment, that some of us buy but hardly use. Such items have a low utility."

Task

You are to examine Sarah's thoughts as expressed above and point out any errors.

Scenario 29: The Difference between Total Utility and Marginal Utility. Just a Dream?

Sabrina studied late in the night for her economics test the following day. She arrived at school early and decided to spend some time reviewing for her test later in the day. She fell asleep and had a dream.

In her dream, she saw a professor reminding her students that total utility is the maximum satisfaction derived from consuming (using) an item, while marginal utility is a measure of the minimum satisfaction derived from using an item. She woke up just in time to rush off to her test.

Task

You are to study the definitions given by the Professor in Sabrina's dream and comment on their correctness.

George and Nathan were in the mall when they looked into a store and noticed a crowd of people shopping. Curious George began the dialogue.

George: I am just curious to know what all those people are doing.

Nathan: What else? Obviously, they are shopping.

George: I know that. But what exactly is their motive? What are they trying to achieve? You know? Their objective?

Nathan: I suppose they have different objectives. Some just love to shop, some are bargain hunters, and some may be just replenishing stocks.

George: I believe there is one common objective that drives the behaviour of all those consumers.

Nathan: Well, I suppose so. But I haven't got a clue as to what it is.

(Thus ended the dialogue).

Task

As a student of microeconomics, and particularly consumer theory, what do economists assume to be the objective of the consumer?

After a lecture on Indifference Curves, students congregate in the cafeteria to further discuss the lecture. The question is this: When is the consumer in a utility maximization position?

After a few minutes of heated debate, the consensus was that the consumer was in equilibrium and maximizing his or her utility when he or she was at a point on the highest indifference curve.

Task

Your task, as a student of microeconomics, is to comment on the consensus reached in the cafeteria.

The College of Bested is located in the town of St. Mary's (both college and town are fictitious, of course). Bested is recognized as having one of the better economics programs in the area.

In one economics class, the students are studying consumer choice using the indifference curve approach. Sam is adamant that indifference curves are linear but downward-sloping because substitutes can be found for just about any good. Donna contends that indifference curves must either be vertical or horizontal, depending on whether the bundles are substitutes or complements.

Task

Your task here is to explain the properties of indifference curves.

The Econ family is known for their knowledge of economics. As a matter of fact, Jack, the second son, often spends time helping college students with their economics. In a recent conversation with his friend Robert, Jack claimed that given a family's budget, the prices of two items, and the marginal utilities associated with the two items, he could determine how much of each item the family should buy in order to maximize its utility.

Task

You are required to use the information provided below to show that Jack's claim is possible.

The price of A is $2 and the price of B is $3, and the budget is $12.

Quantity of A	MUA	MUA/PA	Quantity of B	MUB	MUB/PB
1	16		1	21	
2	18		2	24	
3	16		3	18	
4	14		4	15	
5	10		5	12	
6	6		6	6	
7	2		7	3	

A group of people are assembled on a Sunday afternoon for a tea party to celebrate the transformation of their small town from a low-income area to an affluent town. Mr. Anderson opened his second-hand shop in the town over 30 years ago when most people in town were low-income earners. Although the majority of people have good reason to celebrate their good fortunes, Mr. Anderson has not benefitted from the economic growth of the town. .

Task

As a student of economics, your task is to explain how Mr. Anderson might deal with the current situation.

PART 3

PRODUCTION AND COST

Mrs. Gwendolyn Jarvis is the owner of this store. Her objective is to maximize her profits from her business. Business is doing so well that Mrs. Jarvis has decided to hire a manager whose salary is related to the revenue of the business.

Task

You are to point out any conflict between the manager and the owner, as far as management decisions are concerned.

Scenario 36: Decisions! Decisions! Decisions! Which method to use?

Penultimate Inc. is a company that manufactures high-quality pens and pencils. The company is faced with the methods of producing pens shown in the following table. The inputs used are capital and labour, and their costs are $5 and $6, respectively. The market price of the pens is $10 each.

Method	Capital	Labour	Output
1	10	6	24
2	15	2	25

Task

Your task in this scenario is to use the available data to determine the method that Penultimate should use to manufacture its pens.

Farmer Macdonald uses land and labour to produce a certain type of vegetable on his farm.

The foreman often talks to the workers in terms of total product, average product, and marginal product of labour, but they have no idea what he is talking about. One outspoken worker admits to the foreman that he does not know what the foreman is talking about, and suggests that he uses pictures to illustrate.

Task

You are required to draw total product (TP), average product (AP), and marginal product (MP) curves so that the workers can have an idea what the foreman is talking about.

Most students seem to be interested in technology and its effect on production. When Professor Tan accepted an invitation to lecture on the effect of technology on production, the lecture hall was full, although some people claimed that the professor was a charlatan. They say it is evidenced by his name. Professor Charl A. Tan was prompt, as usual. After a short welcome, the professor went straight into his lecture. The highlight of the evening occurred when the professor claimed that modern technology affected only marginal product and average product, but not total product. At that point, many hands were raised, and many throats were cleared, but Professor Tan recognized no one. The lecture ended with Professor Tan thanking the audience for attending.

Task

You are to comment on Professor Tan's claim that modern technology does not affect total product.

You have known of students forming study groups and you have heard of the benefits of such groups, but you have no personal experience with them because you have never joined one, that is, until now. Your friend, who has a really good grasp of economics, invited you to join a new study group that she was forming. You consented. In class, you were studying the principle of substitution, so at the first meeting of the group, the group leader suggested that you pay attention to the following problem:

A business enterprise can substitute labour for capital or capital for labour in its production process. Developments in the market for machinery have resulted in a significant reduction in the cost of machines in general. The objective of the business enterprise is to produce any given volume of output at a minimum cost. How should the business respond to this reduction in the cost of machines?

Task

Answer the question posed in the above paragraph.

Scenario 40: Professor Noce Comments on the Law of Diminishing Returns

You probably remember Professor Noce from the economics department at Nosuch University of Noneconomic Science (see Scenario 21). While walking to his office one sunny day, he noticed a few of his students studying on the lawn. As his custom was, he stopped to inquire what they were studying. They responded that they were studying the law of diminishing returns.

Before continuing the journey to his office, Professor Noce offered the following piece of information:

"There are three important points that you need to note about the law of diminishing returns:

1. *The law applies to the long run since it mentions <u>eventually</u> or <u>after a while.</u>*
2. *The law applies only to agriculture where land is scarce, in an economic sense.*
3. *Diminishing returns begin immediately after the total product is maximized.*

If you can keep these three points in mind, you will understand the law of diminishing returns a lot better. Do enjoy the day."

Task

You are to examine the three points noted by Professor Noce and comment on them.

Scenario 41: You Had a Dream—A Conference of Economists

You went to bed thinking of the economics test you had early the following morning. You fell asleep before long, and you had the most amazing dream. In that dream, you were at a conference convened to discuss contributors to production and cost theory. In attendance were several renowned economists. An official who appeared to be the chairman of the conference was seated at a table with six other distinguished persons, all with microphones in front of them.

After the usual preliminaries, it was agreed that participants would be identified only by their initials. The first person to speak was introduced as D. R. He looked something like the following photograph. Someone next to me whispered that he was indistinguishable from David Ricardo.

Born: 1772

Died: 1823

Interest at conference: Law of Diminishing Returns

He said that he was there to review the Law of Diminishing Returns.

Next to speak was A.M. He resembled the photo below. Before A.M. could utter his first words, a young conference attendant, unable to restrain herself, shouted, "That's Alfred Marshall, I recognize him."

Born: 1842

Died: 1924

Interest at conference: Demand, Supply, and Elasticity

He made it quite clear that he was at the conference to ensure that no one "messes" (his word) with his doctrine that demand and supply determine value.

The next speaker arose amid thunderous applause when the name F. K. was called. The loudest applause came from a group who called themselves the Chicago School. I was able to take the following snapshot of him. Doesn't he look like Frank Knight?

Born: 1885

Died: 1972

Interest at conference: Production, especially investment

He admitted that he attended the conference mainly to reconnect with some of his friends at the University of Chicago.

The next speaker rose slowly to his feet after hearing his name, J. V. He looked across the room, recognized a few faces, and then shook hands with F. K. who was seated next to him. A young enthusiastic Canadian economist stood up and waived a sign with some U-shaped curves on it, shouting, "He is Canadian. I know him. He is Jacob Viner.

Born: 1892

Died: 1970

Interest at conference: Cost curves

According to J. V, he attended the conference to see what developments had been made with respect to short-run and long-run cost curves.

A venerable elderly man rose to the name of A. S. Because of his stature among economists, the chairman was allowed to refer to him as Adam Smith. There were several photographs like the one below all over the room.

Born: 1723

Died: 1790

Interest at conference: Developments in production theory

Adam Smith expressed his pleasure at seeing so many economists at the conference but wondered what advances had been made since his work on the *division on labour*.

The next speaker was announced as G. S. An economist sitting next to me was quite certain that she knew him and that he was none other than George Stigler. In support of her claim, she pulled the following picture from her wallet.

Born: 1911

Died: 1991

Interest at conference: Neoclassical production

G. S. remarked how happy he was to see that real data were being used to support theory, and encouraged researchers to continue the practice.

The next speaker stood to his feet after the chairman announced that he needed no introduction. He did not give his name but the tee-shirt he wore under his jacket bore a big c. He explained that the **C** stood for *capitalism*. The audience responded with shouts of approval. I was familiar with his facial profile, having seen it on many occasions although I could not remember exactly where or when. Someone whispered that he was Milton Friedman. He looked a great deal like this:

Born: 1912

Died: 2006

Interest at conference: Free enterprise system

After the chairman managed to restore order, the speaker announced that he was delighted to see so many of his colleagues at the conference. He encouraged them to continue the struggle against government intervention in the economy.

The chairman of the conference got up to say something when the alarm on my cell phone awoke me. It was then that I realized that it was all a dream.

Task

Reflect on your dream.

Scenario 42: This train is bound for Salem and Plymouth. Special production function

Imagine that you are on a train travelling from Salem to Plymouth in Massachusetts. Seated in front of you are two well-dressed gentlemen. They seem to be well acquainted with each other and likely travelling together. You hear them talking about their time at Amherst College, and how they collaborated on a production function.

Task

You are to hazard a guess as to who these two gentlemen might be.

Scenario 43: Keep an eye on those inventories. They are crucial in production planning

The CEO of the Aware Corporation is very keen on inventory levels. His supervisors and managers lovingly refer to him as Sir Inventories because of his emphasis on inventories in the production process. At a monthly planning meeting of the production department of the Aware Corporation, the following agenda was proposed:

Agenda

1. Adoption of the agenda
2. Minutes of the previous meeting
3. Reports
4. Inventory
5. Next meeting
6. Adjournment

The meeting proceeded smoothly until they came to item #4—Inventory. The CEO spoke at some length about the importance of inventories in signaling the direction of production. He was particularly upset that the report on inventories was not ready at the time of the meeting. According to him, "Our inventories speak to us."

Task

You are to explain why unplanned changes in inventories are so important for the production planning process.

Carolyn Baker owns and manages a bakery, supplying bread, cakes, pastries, and so on, to retail outlets. She operates from an old building that she converted into a bakery. She owns the building and therefore pays no rent. A similar building nearby is rented for $ 15,000 a year. A major bakery with business establishments from coast to coast has offered Carolyn a long-term contract to manage its national operation. If she accepts the offer, her salary will be $ 120,000 annually. Before making her decision, Carolyn sat down with her accountant to review her own business results, which are presented below and are typical of the last several years.

Total revenue	$320 000
Total expenses	$200 000
Total profits	$120 000

Carolyn does not draw a salary, so she considers her profit of $ 120,000 to be her salary.

Task

Assuming other things, such as taxes and job satisfaction, are equal, you are to determine whether or not Carolyn should accept the offer.

Scenario 45: Algebra Can Help Us to get from Total to Average, even when talking about cost

Cathy and Eugene (Remember them from Scenario 13?) have been studying together since the beginning of the semester and the partnership has really paid dividends for these two students. In their case, the saying that two heads are better than one is exemplified, or as they say, 'iron sharpens iron.' These two exemplary students are meeting at the university library to discuss (quietly, of course) a lecture just given by Professor Query.

Professor Query had taught that once you have the total cost of producing a given quantity of output, it is relatively easy to derive the average cost. As hard as they try, neither Cathy nor Eugene can illustrate algebraically that average total cost (ATC) = Average fixed cost (AFC) + Average variable cost (AVC). In utter frustration, they decide to pay a visit to Professor Query during his office hours.

Task

Your task in this scenario is to illustrate algebraically that ATC = AFC + AVC. Is it as simple as the professor had claimed?

One afternoon, after Calvin's economics class, he decided to pass by his father's office to get a ride home. His father, an economist by profession, was interested in what his son was doing at college, so he requested to see his notes. Surprisingly, this is what he saw:

Notes on cost unit curves

1. All unit cost curves are U-shaped
2. The minimum point of the average total cost curve occurs at a lower level of output than that of the average variable cost curve
3. The marginal cost curve cuts the average fixed cost curve at its minimum point
4. The average total cost curve and the average variable cost curve are parallel

Astonished at what he had seen, the father shook his head and remarked: "No wonder what his name spells if read from right to left."

Task

You are to review the son's notes above and point out the errors, if any.

Games can be used effectively as learning devices. Suppose there is a game called *Parade of Marginals* designed to help students in introductory microeconomics learn and remember the concept of *marginal*. The game involves writing down as many marginal concepts used in introductory microeconomics as you can. The player with the most marginal concepts after the time allotted wins the game.

Task

Your task is to play the game. In addition to writing down as many marginal concepts as you can, you are required to define each concept written down. Go ahead and play the game.

Scenario 48: Meeting at the Restaurant—Economies of Scale?

Thinkecon (not a real company) is a prestigious private economics consulting organization that offers economic advice mainly to large corporations. You have been employed by Thinkecon as an economic adviser mainly in the area of cost control. The manager of a large restaurant chain (Food Sense) has approached Thinkecon with a request for a meeting to discuss an assignment related to controlling costs at Food Sense.

It is a well-known fact that many important business decisions are made during meals at restaurants. Some say it's the wine rather than the food. In any event, it was agreed that the meeting would take place at a Food Sense Restaurant, not unlike the one pictured below.

Task

You are to explain why it might make good business sense for Food Sense to centralize its purchasing rather than having each restaurant ordering its own supplies.

Scenario 49: Economic Concept Explains Panasonic's Product Offering

Panasonic produces TV sets, telephone systems, cameras, DVD players, home appliances, tools, computers, security products, and so on. Your friend claims that there is neither rhyme nor reason behind Panasonic's product offering.

Task

Your task is to indicate the economic concept that can be used to explain Panasonic's product offering.

You: Hi Dad!

Father: Hi! How was school today?

You: It was great, especially our economics class.

Father: What did you talk about?

You: It was so interesting. We spoke about economies of scope. You know when companies produce different products together. You know how you have always said that firms should always specialize and focus on what they know best? Well, I learned today that it may not be always good.

Father: I don't know what kind of economics you are studying, but I know that if a firm does not concentrate on the one or two products that it is best at producing, it could be heading for serious trouble. It's just not good to dabble in all kinds of products.

You: Dad, let me explain.

Father: Yes. Go ahead and explain. I can hardly wait.

Task

You are to explain to your father, from an economic perspective, why it may be a good idea to produce different goods together than to produce separately.

PART 4

MARKET STRUCTURE AND PRICING

Imagine that your rich uncle took you to *Fantasy Island* on a vacation. There you noticed a market type with the following features:

1. A large number of firms
2. Homogeneous products
3. No entry or exit barriers
4. Knowledge of the market

During your entire visit, you have not heard or seen a single competitive advertisement.

Task

You are required to explain why the firms in pure competition do not engage in competitive advertising.

(The following dialogue took place between two friends, Mr. Ambrose and Mr. Benjamin.)

Mr. Ambrose: Good morning Ben. Isn`t it a lovely morning?

Mr. Benjamin: Good morning to you too, Amby. It sure is a beautiful morning. I am sure you've heard of the government's plan to employ an economist to advise it on pricing policy for firms in perfect competition. The objective they claim is to keep prices as low as possible.

Mr. Ambrose: Oh yes. I heard about it. I don't particularly like the idea of government intervening in price setting. I don't suppose anyone does, but I don't object to any policy designed to keep prices affordable. However, I really don't see the advantage of hiring the economist.

Mr. Benjamin: I am not quite sure how such things work, but I suppose the government has sought the advice of experts who know about such things.

Mr. Ambrose: Politicians quite often don't follow the advice of their economic advisers. They are more interested in what brings them votes.

Mr. Benjamin: Amby, I see what you mean. There are many more consumers than there are firms, so by keeping prices low, the government would be making more people happy.

Mr. Ambrose: That's right Ben. It has nothing to do with good pricing policy. It's just a vote grabber. Think about it Ben. The government is just trying to gain popularity.

Mr. Benjamin: It seems as if you are saying that the government is just implementing tactics in order to be popular with consumers. I personally think that the policy will help me because my annual income as a semi-retired literary agent is less than $40,000. But I can see why a rich lawyer like you, with an annual income of more than $200,000, would oppose the policy.

Mr. Ambrose: My opposition is not to the employment of the economist. I am all in favour of helping consumers, especially less fortunate ones. Ben, you know I have helped people in this community. My opposition is to the purpose for which the economist is hired. It is not a good use of public funds.

Mr. Benjamin: O.K., Amby.

Mr. Ambrose: O.K., Ben. See you later.

Task

You are required to explain why it is unnecessary and even wasteful to employ someone to advise on pricing policy in pure competition

Scenario 53: To Advertise or not to advertise. Hard choice

Fashion Boutique is a small retail store that sells women's clothes. Fashion Boutique operates in an industry that is as close as possible to pure competition. For all practical purposes, it is a purely competitive firm. It is a price-taker and a quantity adjuster. An advertising agent approaches Fashion Boutique and offers to advertise its products at a 40% discount on the regular advertising rate.

Task

In this scenario, you are to decide whether or not Fashion Boutique should accept the agent's offer.

Scenario 54: If it's not earning a profit, shut it down. That is Professor Charl A. Tan's motto

A certain firm is operating with fixed costs. The price of its product is $10 and it has no control over this price. The firm's average total cost (ATC) is below the given price of $10, thus the firm is earning a profit. Its lowest average variable cost (AVC) is $6. Changes in the market for this firm's product suddenly caused its price to fall to $8, which is below the firm's ATC. The firm is now incurring losses. Professor Charl A. Tan (see Scenario 38) was consulted on the matter. His advice: Shut it down.

Task

As a student of microeconomics, you are to examine the situation and then decide whether or not the professor is right.

Scenario 55: Tough decision at Loose Leaf

When Leonard Brooks opened Loose Leaf Binding Company, it was the only one in town. His business flourished, and profits were high. He charged a reasonable price. As the town's population grew, more loose-leaf-binding companies emerged. The increase in the number of companies forced the price down, but Mr. Brooks was still earning a profit. More firms entered the industry until no firm was making a profit, and no one had control over the price. They were all just breaking even. Mr. Brooks decided to stay in the business.

Task

You are to study Mr. Brooks' case and determine if he made the right choice.

Scenario 56: Who knows the answer? Pareto optimality

The professor always starts his class with a question, and he identifies the student he wants to answer. He says that is a way of keeping his students on their toes.

This morning the question is: what is Pareto optimality?

Task

Your task is to answer the professor's question.

Scenario 57: Utterly confused. Is it useful?

Your study group (Scenario 39) has been extremely helpful. Currently, you are studying the purely competitive model. One member of the group has this to say:

"I understand the purely competitive model, but it is absolutely useless. You can't even find a single example of pure competition in the real world. It just does not exist. Talk about straw man. In the real world, firms produce items that are not homogenous, they do have some control over their prices, and freedom of entry and exit is nothing but a myth. To be totally honest, that model is useless. Studying it is a waste of time."

Task

Your task for this scenario is to defend the purely competitive model by showing that it is useful.

Scenario 58: Protection available?

Tropical Pharmaceuticals, Inc. (a hypothetical company) has developed a drug that has proved to be successful in treating migraine headaches. Tropical Pharmaceuticals wants to ensure that other pharmaceutical companies will not duplicate its product.

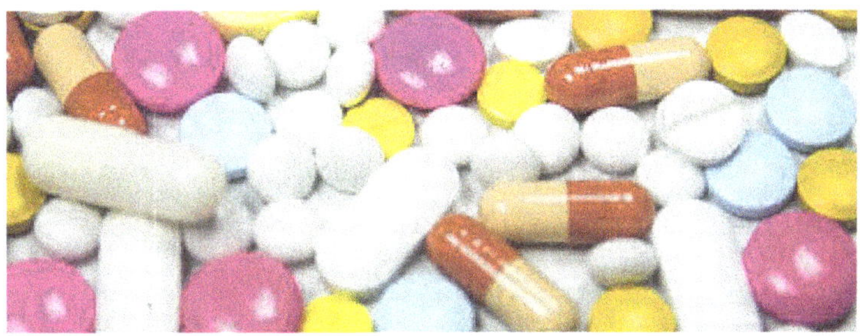

Your friend insists that there is nothing that Tropical Pharmaceuticals can do in this matter because it's a free country.

Task

Your task is to prove that your friend is wrong by suggesting a means whereby Tropical Pharmaceuticals can prevent other pharmaceutical companies from duplicating its product.

Scenario 59: Presentation at the Monopoly Convention

Each year, economists of all persuasions meet in different parts of the world for a monopoly convention. This year, the meeting is scheduled to be held in New Orleans, and your boss, a business economist who is an expert on monopoly theory, has accepted an invitation to deliver a paper on monopoly theory. Below is an audience similar to the one that your boss will be addressing.

As her assistant, your boss has asked you to prepare a section of her presentation dealing with natural monopoly.

Task

Your task is to prepare a document of about 150 words on natural monopoly so that your boss can include it in her presentation.

On your way home from work, you turned on the car radio and heard Professor Ecnud just finishing up an interview. Below are his closing remarks:

"So remember these points:

1. The short-run is any period less than a year
2. The long-run is any period more than one year and less than five years
3. The very long run is any period exceeding five years

Some might want to tell you that these 'runs' refer to the firm's ability to vary its inputs but don't be fooled by them. Thanks for having me on the program."

Task

Since you are a student of microeconomics, you are required to comment on Professor Ecnud's closing remarks.

All the electricity in a small town is provided by a private electricity generating company known as Total Electricity. This company charges a fixed price per day for its electricity. Through thorough analysis, Total Electricity has determined that its profit-maximization price (rate) is $0.70 per day. Instead of charging $0.70 per day, the company charges $0.65 per day. Many people who know of this practice claim the Total Electricity is behaving irrational.

Task

Your task for this scenario is to answer the following question:

Is there any rationale in Total Electricity's pricing policy?

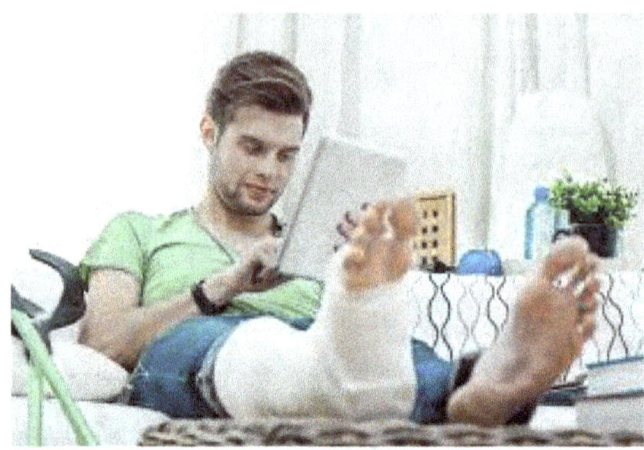

You twisted your ankle while running. After examining your ankle at the hospital, the doctor recommended that you stay at the hospital for a day or two for observation. You have an economics test in one week, and you just have to study. Your girlfriend has offered to help by quizzing you. Here are the questions that she asked:

1. What is the shape of the demand curve for a firm in pure competition?
2. If a firm in pure competition is operating where the price is below average total cost but above average variable cost, it is incurring losses and should close down. Indicate whether true or false.

   True [ ]   False [ ]

3. Which of the following is true of pure competition?
   a) Each firm determines the price at which it sells its product
   b) Each firm tries to differentiate its product
   c) A few firms compete fiercely for customers
   d) Each firm is a price-taker and a quantity-adjuster
4. "A profit-seeking monopolist will always charge the highest possible price for its product." Discuss.
5. What is price discrimination?

Task

You are required to do the quiz.

Born: October 31, 1903	Born: May 18, 1899
Died: August 5, 1983	Died: July 16, 1967
Book: The Economics of Imperfect Competition	Book: The Theory of Monopolistic Competition

Task

In this scenario are pictured two economists. Your task is to identify them.

Scenario 64: Name that Market Structure

It was your first trip to Althealand (a fictitious country), and one of the first things you noticed was an abundance of independent flower shops. On practically every corner in the capital city, there is a flower shop not unlike the one pictured below.

You noticed that there were slight variations in prices from one flower shop to another, their products were differentiated, and competitive advertising among them was fierce.

Task

On the basis of the information given above, you are required to identify the market type in which Althealand's flower shops operate.

Scenario 65: Different strokes for different taxis

Cross-Town Taxi Service finds that increasing numbers of taxi companies have entered the industry. One keen observer commented that they may look different but they were all the same.

Task

You are required to suggest ways whereby Cross-Town Taxi might set itself apart from other taxi companies in the field.

Scenario 66: Advertising to the Rescue. We Love Chocolate

In November 2006, Hershey Canada Inc. voluntarily recalled a wide range of its chocolate products nationwide after salmonella bacteria were detected in some of its candies. Doubtlessly, this recall adversely affected Hershey's candy sales in Canada.

Task

Your task is to answer the following question:

What kind of advertising should Hershey have engaged in to attempt to rectify this situation?

Scenario 67: Oligopoly—No General Theory Here

Because of your expertise on economic matters, you have been invited to appear on a popular TV show called, *Anything Goes*. After discussing several economic issues, someone asked why there were so many models of oligopoly behaviour. Because you are knowledgeable in this area, the host turned to you for a response.

Task

You are required to provide an answer to the question raised in the scenario.

(Roger and William are having breakfast in the cafeteria when the following conversation ensues).

Roger: Did you know that the rapid increase in the price of houses was due to the government's attempt promote competition?

William: Where did you get that information?

Roger: It's right here on the Internet.

William: Really? Let's see.

Roger: Here it is.

(They read)

"For the past 20 years, house prices have risen only very slightly. Last year, the government introduced new measures to promote competition and to reduce monopoly power. Patents and franchises seem to be things of the past and financial and tax incentives are easily given to small businesses. Not coincidently, since last year, the prices of houses began to rise rapidly. It therefore does not take much to conclude that the rapid increase in the prices of houses was due to the government's attempt to promote competition."

Roger: It must be true. It's right there on the Internet.

William: I guess so.

Task

Your task is to use this scenario to show that just because something is on the Internet does not mean that it's true.

Scenario 69: A Kink in the Demand Curve? Oops! How Can This Be? Look at the Assumptions

(Classroom setting with Professor Query, Eugene, Cathy, and other students)

Professor: Well then, according to Paul Sweezy Robert Hall and Charles Hitch, the demand curve of a firm in oligopoly may have a kink.

Cathy: What is the cause of the kink?

Professor: Well, two assumptions will cause a kink. Can anyone tell us what these assumptions are?

Eugene: Yes. A price increase by one firm will not be matched by a similar increase by other firms, and a reduction in price by one firm will be matched by a similar reduction in other firms.

Professor: That's right.

Student: The assumptions make sense. It's only logical.

Professor: Does the MR = MC rule for profit maximization still hold?

Cathy: I think it still holds.

Student: I also think the rule still holds.

Professor: O.K. Great! Note that it's the "kinked" (not "kinky") demand curve. Your assignment, class, is to explain the implication of a kinked demand curve for price rigidity.

Task

Your task is to do Professor Query's assignment.

Scenario 70: Perplexing Questions about the Kink. Study Group to the Rescue

You are perplexed about certain aspects of the kinked demand curve, so you decide to bring your concerns to your study group. Specifically, your concerns are:

1. The model does not tell us where the kink occurs
2. The model does not tell us how the rigid price is established in the first place

Your study group decides to take your concerns to Professor Query.

Task

Your task is to predict what Professor Query will say.

Scenario 71: Causes of Price Rigidity in Oligopoly Markets

In a certain industry, you noticed that there were only a few firms and that they seemed to be interdependent. You noticed that small changes in cost were not reflected in the price of the product.

Task

Your task is to explain why prices may be rigid even when there are small changes in cost.

Scenario 72: A Class Project—Cost-plus Pricing

In your microeconomics class, each student is required to write a short note on one aspect of market structure. Different topics such as purely competitive pricing, supply curve of a purely competitive firm, causes of monopoly, market types, characteristics of monopolistic competition, oligopoly pricing, cartels, etc. were written on pieces of paper and placed in a box from which each student drew a topic without being able to see inside the box. When it was your turn, you drew cost-plus pricing.

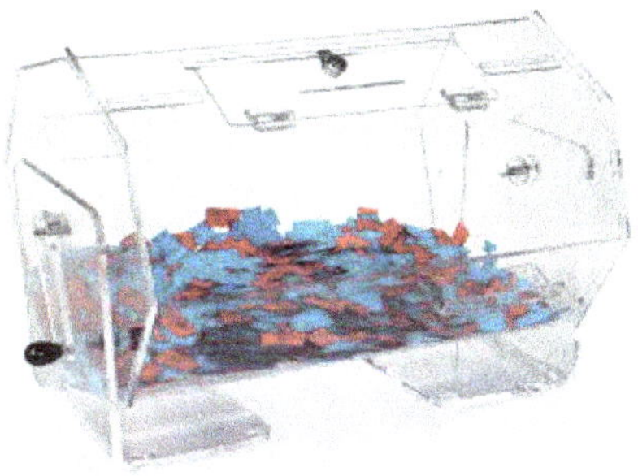

Task

Your task is to write a short note (about 120 words) on the advantages and disadvantages of cost-plus pricing.

PART 5

INTERNATIONAL TRADE

WebPro designs web pages mainly for Canadian businesses. In a recent visit to India, Mr. Greene, the owner of WebPro discovered that webpage designers in India could design web pages to his specifications at a fraction of the cost that he paid in Canada.

Mr. Greene is wondering how he might take advantage of the relatively cheap labour in India.

Task

You are required to suggest a means whereby Mr. Greene can benefit from low labour cost in India.

Scenario 74: Tariffs? A Great Way for a Country to earn Income

You have been studying for a while so you decided to take a break. You turned on the TV and used the remote control to see if you could find anything interesting. Flipping through the channels, you noticed a panel discussion on taxes on imported goods.

Although you were looking for something more relaxing, you paused to hear and see what the participants were saying. One member of the panel asked another member whether or not tariffs were good for the importing country. The member questioned responded that tariffs were indeed good for the country but declined to explain for lack of time. Your interest was aroused because you had never paid much attention to tariffs. You decided to research the topic.

Task

Your task is to write a short statement on the negative effects of tariffs.

Scenario 75: Currency Tied to Oil?

Oilando (an imaginary country) is well endowed with huge oil reserves scattered all over the country. Undercan (another imaginary country) is a close neighbour of Oilando. Both countries have very close economic ties. Undercan buys the vast majority of Oilando's oil exports, and most of Oilando's imports come from Undercan. Oilando has a flexible exchange rate system.

The demand for oil is known to be highly inelastic which means that a change in the price of oil has negligible effect on the quantity demanded. It has been observed over the years that whenever the price of oil rises, the value of the Oilando dollar in terms of the Undercan dollar rises as well. This is true for more than 90% of the time.

Task

Your task in this scenario is to explain why the value of the Oilando dollar rises in terms of the Undercan dollar when the price of oil rises.

Scenario 76: How Much Does It Cost? Can I Afford It? It's British. That Depends on the Exchange Rate

A Canadian by the name of David spent a year in England and fell in love with the land rover, a British car. On his return to Canada, he decided to purchase a land rover. He learned from a Canadian land rover dealer that the car he wanted would cost £35,000. The maximum amount of money that David was willing to spend on the car was $65,000 CAD. The exchange rate between the British £ and the CAD$ was £1 = CAD $1.95.

Task

Your task is to determine:

1. If David can afford to buy the car
2. What the exchange rate would have to be to enable him to afford the car.

Scenario 77: To Flex or Not to Flex: Advantages and Disadvantages of Flexible Exchange Rates

Your study group has been doing really well. It demonstrates that "iron sharpens iron". The advantages of the *division of labour* are exemplified in your study group. You are now studying exchange rates and in the usual lottery, you drew the *advantages and disadvantages of flexible exchange rates.*

Task

Your task is to prepare notes on the *Advantages and Disadvantages of Flexible Exchange Rates* to be distributed to your study group.

PART 6

SAMPLE TESTS

Answer All Questions   Time Allowed: I hour & 15 min.

PART 1: DEFINITIONS (10 MARKS)

1. Define each of the following terms. (Give an example if possible)

(a) Social science
(b) Positive statement
(c) Rent
(d) Production possibility (p-p) schedule
(e) Product market

PART 2: MULTIPLE-CHOICE (20 MARKS)

Select the letter that corresponds with the correct answer.

2. Which of the following is true about the study of economics?

a. It is guaranteed to make you rich

b. It helps you to think logically

c. It guarantees that you will always be able to find a job

d. You will have a perfect understanding of how the economy of any country works.

3. Economists work in:

a. private firms such as banks and large manufacturing companies

b. colleges and universities

c. international organizations such as the World Bank

d. all of the above

4. Which of the following is scarce (in a relative sense) even in a land flowing with milk and honey? (Jorobel?)

a. Natural resources such as rivers and lakes
b. Human resources
c. Capital such as roads and equipment
d. All of the above

5. Profit is the income earned from:

a. financial capital

b. entrepreneurial services

c. real capital

d. land

6. The scientific method or approach involves:

a. Observation and measurement

b. Verification through testing

c. The formulation of hypotheses

d. All of the above

7. An economic model is:

a. just like a real economy in all respects

b. a simplified version of a real economy

c. always very easy to understand

d. none of the above

8. A hypothesis is:

a. a statement that is known to be true
b. the same as a normative statement
c. a statement that can be verified by testing
d. always stated in mathematical terms

9. Which of the following is true of positive statements?

a. They refer to facts

b. They deal with what is, was, or will be

c. They can be verified

d. All of the above

10. The main difference between positive statements and normative statements is that:

a. positive statements are always true while normative statements may be true or false

b. positive statements can be verified while normative statements cannot be verified

c. positive statements are based on emotions while normative statements are based on facts

d. positive statements are a part of economic study while normative statements are not.

11. Which of the following is true?

a. A stock is a constant while a flow is a variable

b. A flow is a constant while a stock is a variable

c. Neither stocks nor flows are variables

d. Stocks and flows are both variables

12. Economists use:

a. only endogenous variables

b. only exogenous variables

c. both endogenous and exogenous variables

d. neither endogenous nor exogenous variables

13. The opportunity cost of an item is:

a. the amount of money it costs to produce the item

b. the amount of money for which the item is sold

c. the best alternative given up in order to get the item

d. all of the above

14. A production possibility diagram shows all of the following <u>except</u>:

a. scarcity

b. choice

c. price

d. opportunity cost

15. If an economy is operating under conditions of increasing opportunity cost, its production possibility (p-p) curve will be:

a. concave and upward-sloping

b. concave and downward sloping

c. linear and upward-sloping

d. linear and downward-sloping

16. Which of the following will cause a country's p-p curve to shift to the right?

a. It acquires better technology

b. It produces a greater quantity of goods and services

c. It uses unemployed resources

d. All of the above

17. Indicate whether the following statement is true or false.

A point that lies above a p-p curve is neither desirable nor attainable.

a. True

b. False

18. If an economy decides to produce more goods and services by using unemployed resources, the opportunity cost of the additional goods and services is:

a. the payment made for the resources that it uses to produce the additional goods and services

b. the cost of producing the additional goods and services

c. nothing

d. the revenue or income received from selling the additional goods and services

19. Which of the following is a microeconomic issue?

a. The level of aggregate production of goods and services in an economy

b. The prices that a firm charges for its products

c. The level of employment in a country

d. The variation of total production in an economy from time to time.

20. Consider the simple circular flow model. In the factor market:

a. the buyers are the firms while the sellers are the households

b. the buyers are the households while the sellers are the firms

c. firms are both buyers and sellers

d. households are both buyers and sellers.

21. In the circular flow model:

a. real flows are money flows

b. real flows are payments for the resources

c. real flows are flows of goods and services and flows of resources

d. there are no money flows.

PART 3: PROBLEMS AND EXERCISES (5 MARKS)

22. Use production possibility diagrams (graphs) to show how each of the following will affect an economy's production possibility curve. Assume that the economy produces furniture (F) and smartphones (S), and that it operates under conditions of **increasing opportunity cost.** <u>Put smartphones on the vertical axis, and furniture on the horizontal axis.</u>

(a) A fall in the prices of furniture and an increase in the prices of smartphones

(b) An increase in technology that positively affects the production of smartphones but not furniture

(c) Workers in the furniture industry are laid off because of a fall in demand for furniture.

(d) Workers are imported into the country to work in the smartphone industry.

(e) The government increases the taxes on the sale of both smartphones and furniture.

PART 4: ESSAY QUESTION (5 MARKS)

23. (a) What is an economic model?

(b) Why do economists construct and use models?

Answer All Questions   Time Allowed: 1 Hour & 15 min.

PART 1: DEFINITIONS (10 MARKS)

1. Define each of the following terms, giving examples, if possible.

(a) Real capital
(b) Flow
(c) Relative scarcity
(d) Endogenous variable
(e) Positive statement

PART 2: MULTIPLE CHOICE (20 MARKS)

Select the letter that corresponds with the correct answer.

2. Scarcity could be eliminated as an economic problem if:

a. people would learn to cooperate instead of compete

b. sufficient new reserves of natural resources were discovered

c. output per hour of human labour were increased one hundredfold

d. none of the above

3. Which aspect of human behavior <u>most</u> concerns the economist?

a. The voting pattern in a society and state government

b. The behavior of people as members of a group or organization

c. The behavior of individuals and groups engaged in the process of production, distribution, and consumption

c. Public attitude towards social issues

4. Economists assume that:

a. resources are unlimited but wants are limited
b. resources are limited but wants are unlimited
c. both resources and wants are unlimited
d. both resources and wants are limited

5. Economics is not a science because:

a. human behaviour cannot be studied scientifically

b. mathematics cannot be used effectively in economics

c. economists cannot conduct controlled experiments

d. none of the above

6. A good economic model is one that:

a. contains as many variables as possible

b. is dependent on sophisticated mathematics

c. successfully and consistently explains or predicts economic events

d. does not need assumptions

7. Choice is a direct result of:

a. ambition
b. scarcity
c. extravagance
d. none of the above.

8. Economists construct models in order to:

a. impress non-economists

b. restrict entry into the economics profession

c. make it easier to understand how a real economy works

d. introduce as many variables as possible into their analysis.

9. Disagreement among economists is due to:

a. the fact that economics is not a science

b. the fact that economic models are often expressed verbally instead of mathematically

c. the fact that some economists just don't understand the complexities of modern mathematics used in economic models

d. the fact that economists have different values, or they may use different economic models to explain the same economic phenomenon.

10. Which of the following is a flow?

a. The number of graduates entering the labour force each year

b. The number of students in the cafeteria at 2:00 p.m. on February 23

c. The amount of money in your purse or wallet

d. All of the above are flow variables

11. If two variables move together in the same direction, they are said to be:

a. endogenous variables

b. directly related

c. exogenous variables

d. inversely related

12. Microeconomics deals with:

a. small and unimportant economic issues only

b. only small economic sectors where only few people are employed

c. the behaviour of individual economic units

d. all of the above

13. Factors of production are:

a. scarce in advanced countries but abundant in poor countries

b. required to produce goods but not services

c. scarce in poor countries but abundant in rich countries

d. scarce in both rich and poor countries

14. Economists classify resources into the following categories:

a. Available, scarce, expensive, and natural

b. Land, labour, capital, and entrepreneurship

c. Artificial, financial, human, and manufactured

d. Natural, imported, limitless, and personal

15. The reward for capital is called:

a. rent

b. interest/dividend

c. wages

d. profit

16. The opportunity cost of an item is:

a. the market price of the item expressed in money

b. the monetary cost of the resources used to produce the item

c. the profit obtained from the sale of the item

d. None of the above

17. A production possibility curve shows:

a. the boundary between combinations of goods/services that are attainable through production and those that are unattainable

b. all combinations of goods/services consumed by the economy

c. the total value of all goods/services produced by the economy

d. all possible ways of producing the economy's output of goods/services

18. A linear (straight line) p-p curve, with corn and books on the axes, implies that:

a. the monetary cost of producing corn equals the monetary cost of producing books

b. the economy can only produce equal quantities of corn and books

c. books and corn are perfect substitutes

d. none of the above

19. A production possibility curve showing increasing opportunity cost is:

a. linear and upward-sloping

b. convex and downward-sloping

c. linear and downward-sloping

d. concave and downward-sloping

20. Which of the following will cause a country's p-p curve to shift to the right?

a. The country acquires more resources

b. The country increases production by hiring previously unemployed workers

c. Prices in the country fall

d. All of the above

21. A situation in which the economy cannot produce more of one commodity without producing less of some other commodity is called:

a. production inability

b. a state of unattainability

c. productive inefficiency

d. productive efficiency

PART 3: PROBLEMS AND EXERCISES (5 MARKS)

22. Use production possibility diagrams (graphs) to show how each of the following will affect an economy's production possibility curve. Assume that the economy produces computers (C) and bread (B), and that it operates under conditions of **increasing opportunity cost**. Put computers on the vertical axis and bread on the horizontal axis.

(a) The country switches some resources from computer production to bread production.

(b) The country discovers resources that can be used **only** in bread production.

(c) Unemployed workers leave the country.

(d) Firms use previously unemployed resources to increase their production of computers and bread.

(e) The economy decides to abandon its production of computers and bread.

23. (a) What is an economic model? (1 mark)

(b) Why do economists construct models? (2 marks)

(c) How can one determine the "goodness" of a model? (2 marks)

Answer All Questions   Time Allowed: 1 hour & 15 min.

PART 1. DEFINITIONS (10 MARKS)

1. Define each of the following terms, giving examples, if possible.

a. Supply curve

b. Price elasticity of demand

c. Budget line

d. Marginal product of labour

e. Variable cost

PART 2. MULTIPLE-CHOICE (20 MARKS)

Select the letter that corresponds with the correct answer.

2. A market can exist without:

a. a physical place

b. A price

c. sellers

d. buyers

3. If the supply curve for pens is upward sloping, then an increase in the price of pens will result in a(n):

a. increase in the supply of pens

b. decrease in the supply of pens

c. increase in the quantity of pens supplied

d. decrease in the quantity of pens supplied.

4. Consider hotdogs and ketchup to be complements. If the price of hotdogs rises, we would expect:

a. an increase in the demand for ketchup

b. a decrease in the demand for ketchup

c. a decrease in the demand for hotdogs

d. both b and c.

5. A 10% fall in the price of an item causes the quantity to rise by 6%. This means that the demand for the item is:

a. inelastic

b. unitary elastic

c. elastic

d. perfectly elastic

6. Which of the following is likely to yield the highest tax revenue?

a. A tax on a product with an elastic demand

b. A tax on a product with an inelastic demand

c. A tax on an inferior good

d. A tax on a product with unitary elastic demand

7. Economists refer to a unit of satisfaction as a:

a. satisfit

b. unisat

c. util

d. none of the above

8. If $MU_A/P_A > MU_B/P_B$:

a. the consumer is maximizing his or her satisfaction

b. the consumer would purchase more of good A

c. the consumer would purchase more of good B

d. we cannot predict what the consumer would do

9. An indifference curve shows combinations of goods that:

a. maximize the consumer's satisfaction

b. the consumer can purchase for the same amount of money

c. give the consumer the same level of satisfaction

d. none of the above

10. A household maximizes satisfaction when:

a. the budget line ceases to move outward

b. the indifference curve ceases to move outward

c. the budget line is tangent to an indifference curve

d. none of the above

11. Technological efficiency refers to:

a. input use without reference to cost

b. the lowest cost of producing a given output

c. the maximum output that the firm can produce

d. the maximum inputs required to produce a given output

12. In economics, the short run refers to:

a. a period not exceeding one year

b. a situation in which the firm has at least one fixed factor

c. a period shorter than three months

d. none of the above

13. If total product is rising, then:

a. average product must be falling

b. average product must be at its maximum

c. marginal product must be positive

d. marginal product must be rising

14. Total product will be at its maximum when:

a. marginal product is at its maximum
b. marginal product is zero
c. average product is zero
d. none of the above

15. The law of diminishing returns states that as increasing quantities of a variable factor are added to a fixed factor:

a. the increase in total product will eventually diminish

b. the total product will diminish

c. the total product will never reach its maximum

d. none of the above

16. For a firm using two factors of production, capital and labour, its optimum input mix occurs when:

a. labour and capital are used in equal amounts

b. the ratio of the marginal product of capital to the marginal product of labour equals the ratio of the price of capital to the price of labour

c. the prices of capital and labour begin to rise and the marginal products of capital and labour begin to fall

d. none of the above

17. A firm's cost function states the relationship between:

a. inputs and output
b. price and cost
c. cost and output
d. none of the above

18. Costs incurred by using factors of production already owned by the firm are called:

a. uncollectable costs

b. implicit costs

c. explicit costs

d. marginal costs

19. When ATC has reached its minimum, we know that:

a. ATC = TFC

b. MC = AVC

c. ATC = MC

d. none of the above

20. A firm is experiencing increasing returns to scale if:

a. output more than doubles when all inputs are doubled

b. long-run average cost (LRAC) increases as the firm expands its scale of operation

c. cost is proportional to output

d. none of the above

21. Economies of scope exist when:

a. the production of complementary products together rather than separately reduces cost

b. the firm pursues a narrow rather than a broad scope

c. the firm decides to take advantage of the opportunity to produce goods separately rather than together

d. none of the above

PART 3. PROBLEMS AND EXERCISES (5 MARKS)

22. Use demand and supply diagrams (graphs) to show the effect of each of the following events on equilibrium price and equilibrium quantity of reading lamps. **(Consider reading lamps as normal goods and assume that other things remain equal).**

a. Enrolment in colleges and universities decreases drastically
b. An announcement by reputable scientists that reading lamps preserve vision
c. A decrease in the cost of producing reading lamps
d. The discovery of a more efficient method of producing reading lamps
e. An overall increase in consumers' income.

PART 4. ESSAY QUESTION (5 MARKS)

23. Which cost curve declines continuously and why?

Answer All Questions   Time Allowed: 1 hour & 15 min.

PART 1. DEFINITIONS

1. Define each of the following terms, giving examples, if possible.

a. Demand schedule

b. Equilibrium quantity

c. Inferior good

d. Income elasticity of demand

e. Cost function

PART 2. MULTIPLE-CHOICE (20 MARKS)

Select the letter that corresponds with the correct answer.

2. The market process refers to:

a. the methods used by merchants to take their products to market

b. the various rules and regulations governing behavior in markets

c. the means by which a government sets the price of an item in the market

d. the process by which buyers and sellers exchange goods and services.

3. Tide and Breeze are substitutes as detergents. If the price of Breeze rises, other things being equal:

a. the quantity of Breeze demanded will fall

b. the demand for Breeze will not be affected

c. the demand for Tide will increase

d. all of the above.

4. If the demand increases, other things being equal, we predict:

a. an increase in price and a decrease in quantity

b. an increase in price and an increase in quantity

c. a decrease in price and an increase in quantity

d. a decrease in price and a decrease in quantity.

5. Which of the following is likely to affect the supply of a product?

a. The cost of resources used to produce the product

b. A change in the technology used to produce the product

c. Weather conditions

d. All of the above.

6 Which of the following is a determinant of the degree of price elasticity of demand for an item?

a. The number and closeness of substitutes

b. The fraction of the budget spent on the item

c. The number of uses the item has

d. All of the above

7. In the very short period (market period), the supply is:

a. perfectly elastic

b. unitary elastic

c. perfectly inelastic

d. none of the above

8. Which of the following statements about utility is *incorrect?*

a. If a good is wanted, it yields utility
b. Total utility depends on price
c. Utility is subjective
d. Utility is a measure of satisfaction

9. The consumption of a free good will continue until:

a. the marginal utility becomes positive

b. the total utility is rising

c. the total utility is falling

d. the marginal utility is zero

10. The consumer will be in equilibrium when she spends her budget in such a way that:

a. the marginal utility per dollar of A equals the marginal utility per dollar of B

b. she cannot increase her satisfaction by rearranging her purchases

c. the ratio of the marginal utilities of the items she buys equals the ratio of the prices of the items

d. all of the above

11. Intersecting indifference curves would mean that:

a. preferences cannot be ordered or ranked

b. the law of diminishing marginal rate of substitution is not applicable

c. the consumer was inconsistent

d. all of the above

12. Economic efficiency exists when the firm:

a. uses many factor inputs

b. maximizes input cost

c. minimizes input cost

d. earns a profit

13. The method of production that has the lowest cost associated with it is said to be:

a. marginally efficient

b. economically efficient

c. technically inefficient

d. none of the above

14. In economics, the long run refers to:

a. a situation in which the firm can vary all its inputs
b. a period longer than one year
c. a period longer than five years
d. none of the above

15. The law of diminishing returns is a:

a. long-run phenomenon

b. short-run phenomenon

c. law that cannot be tested

d. hypothesis that is valid in some places but not in others

16. Which of the following is correct?

a. Economic costs = accounting costs + implicit costs

b. Accounting costs = implicit costs + economic costs

c. Accounting costs = all opportunity costs

d. None of the above

17. Which of the following is correct?

a. The MC curve cuts the ATC curve and the AVC curve at the same level of output

b. The MC curve always lies above the AVC curve

c. If MC is rising, then the average cost must also be rising

d. The MC curve cuts the ATC curve and the AVC curve at their minimum points

18. The long-run average cost (LRAC) curve represents:

a. the sum of all the firm's short-run cost curves

b. the firm's cost structure for any period in excess of one year

c. the lowest unit cost at which the firm can produce its output when all factors are variable

d. all of the above

19. If MC is above ATC, then:

a. AFC will rise

b. AVC is declining

c. ATC will rise

d. ATC is falling

20. Decreasing returns to scale can result from:

a. greater specialization of labour and capital

b. large quantity input purchases resulting in quantity discounts

c. the greater efficiency of larger plants

d. inefficiency in management as the operation expands

21. Economies of scope exist when:

a. the production of complementary products together rather than separately reduces cost

b. the firm pursues a narrow rather than a broad scope

c. the firm decides to take advantage of the opportunity to produce goods separately rather than together

d. none of the above

PART 3. PROBLEMS AND EXERCISES (5 MARKS)

22. Use demand and supply diagrams (graphs) to show the effect of each of the following events on equilibrium price and equilibrium quantity of pencil cases. **(Consider pencil cases as normal goods and assume that other things remain equal).**

a. The government provides pens and pencils free of charge to elementary and high school students

b. An increase in the number of students going to school

c. An increase in the number of firms producing and selling pencil cases

d. An increase in the prices of material used to produce pencil cases

e. A significant decrease in the prices of pens and pencils.

PART 4. ESSAY QUESTION (5 MARKS)

23. What reasons can you give for the existence of increasing returns to scale and decreasing returns to scale?

Answer All Questions   Time Allowed: 1 Hour & 15 min.

PART 1. DEFINITIONS (10 MARKS)

1. Define each of the following terms

a. Pure competition

b. Marginal revenue

c. Barriers to entry

d. Duopoly

e. Product differentiation

PART 2. MULTIPLE-CHOICE (20 MARKS)

2. An industry is:

a. a company

b. any business that is not owned by the government

c. a group of firms that produce similar products

d. a group of firms that produce vastly different products

3. Which of the following is true of pure competition?

a. Each firm determines the price at which it sells its product

b. Each firm tries to differentiate its product

c. A few firms compete fiercely for customers

d. Each firm is a price-taker and a quantity-adjuster

4. To maximize its profits, a firm in pure competition will:

a. set its price low enough to attract customers

b. produce a level of output at which price equals marginal cost

c. engage in competitive advertising to attract customers

d. raise its price to increase its revenue

5. The short-run shut-down point occurs at an output level at which:

a. marginal cost equals average total cost

b. price equals average total cost

c. average fixed cost is at a minimum

d. marginal cost equals average variable cost

6. The long-run supply (LRS) curve of a constant-cost industry is:

a. upward sloping

b. horizontal

c. downward sloping

d. non-existent

7. In long-run competitive equilibrium:

a. each firm earns positive economic profits

b. all firms incur slight losses

c. each firm operates where price equals average cost

d. none of the above

8. Monopolies can exist in the long run because:

a. there are barriers to entry into the industry

b. they do not produce at the point where marginal revenue = marginal cost

c. the long run is defined as a situation in which competition does not exist

d. they minimize cost rather than maximize profits

9. Which of the following is true of a monopolist?

a. If marginal revenue is positive, demand is elastic

b. If marginal revenue is zero, demand is unitary elastic

c. If marginal revenue is negative, demand is inelastic

d. All of the above

10. At its present level of output, a monopolist finds that its marginal revenue is greater than its marginal cost. To maximize profits, the monopolist should:

a. reduce price and leave output unchanged

b. increase price and leave output unchanged

c. continue to operate at current price and output levels

d. reduce price and increase output

11. Monopoly tends to:

a. reduce consumer surplus and increase producer surplus

b. increase consumer surplus and reduce producer surplus

c. reduce both consumer and producer surplus

d. increase both consumer and producer surplus

12. Price discrimination is the practice of:

a. refusing to sell to ethnic minority groups

b. adopting a very conservative approach to pricing

c. setting price above average revenue for certain classes of buyers

d. none of the above

13. If a sales tax is imposed on each unit of an item sold by a profit-maximizing monopolist:

a. the price will rise by an amount less than the tax

b. the price will rise by an amount greater than the tax

c. the marginal cost will not be affected

d. neither the price nor the quantity will be affected

14. In monopolistic competition:

a. two monopolists compete against each other
b. some firms in the industry are monopolies while others are purely competitive
c. the firms interchange their roles as pure competitors and pure monopolists
d. many firms produce differentiated products

15. In short-run equilibrium, a firm in monopolistic competition, seeking to maximize its profits, will operate where:

a. marginal revenue exceeds marginal cost

b. marginal revenue equals marginal cost

c. price equals marginal cost

d. price is less than average total cost

16. In long-run equilibrium, a monopolistic competitor will have:

a. price equal to marginal cost

b. price equal to average cost

c. price greater than average cost

d. price less than average cost

17. One major characteristic of firms in oligopoly is that:

a. they produce identical products

b. they all have kinked demand curves

c. they always collude to control price and output

d. they recognize their interdependence

18. An industry with only two firms is called:

a. a double monopoly
b. a duopoly
c. a cartel
d. none of the above

19. Which of the following is a possible explanation of rigid prices?

a. A kinked demand curve

b. Small menu costs

c. Long-term contracts

d. All of the above

20. Concentration ratios show:

a. the percentage of total industry supply accounted for by a few of the largest firms in the industry

b. the ratio of total revenue to total cost

c. the profit ratio within the oligopolistic industry

d. none of the above

21. A market is *contestable* when:

a. it is monopolized

b. the firms in the industry are all oligopolists

c. entry into the market is easy

d. none of the above

PART 3. PROBLEMS AND EXERCISES (5 MARKS)

22. Answer the following questions on the basis of the following diagram. The firm operates in monopolistic competition.

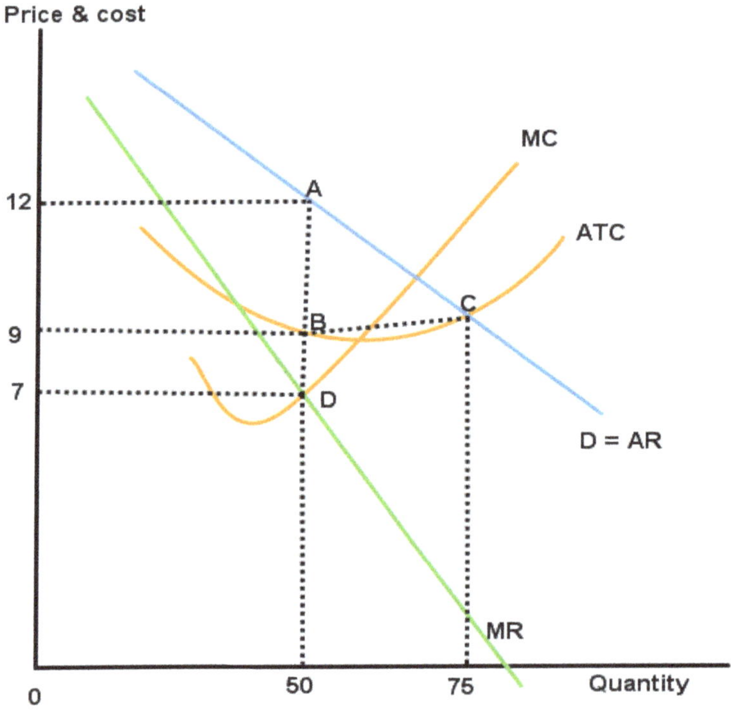

A. What quantity of output should the firm produce in order to maximize profits?

b. What price should the firm charge?

c. What is the maximum profit this firm can make?

d. If this firm charges a price of $9, what will be its total revenue?

e. If this firm raises its price from $9 to $12, its total revenue will ______(rise, fall)

PART 4. ESSAY (5 MARKS)

23. "The objective of the firm is to maximize its profits. If this objective is achieved, the firm is in equilibrium. The firm cannot, therefore, be in equilibrium if it is not making a profit." Discuss this statement.

Answer All Questions   Time Allowed: 1 Hour & 15 min.

PART 1. DEFINITIONS (10 MARKS)

1. Define each of the following terms:

a. price-taker

b. Pareto optimality

c. price discrimination

d. collusion

e. workable competition

PART 2. MULTIPLE-CHOICE (20 MARKS)

2. A purely competitive market is one in which:

a. competitive advertising is rampant

b. demand plays no part in pricing

c. firms unite to fix the price

d. each firm is a quantity adjuster

3. A purely competitive firm:

a. can set its own price

b. is one among many

c. has no control over quantity

d. cannot easily enter the industry

4. Which of the following is true of a firm in pure competition?

a. It can never earn a profit
b. It adjusts quantity to maximize profits
c. It sets its price to maximize profits
d. It differentiates its products

5. The short-run supply curve of a purely competitive firm is:

a. its average variable cost curve

b. its entire average total cost curve

c. the section of its marginal cost curve that lies above its average total cost curve

d. the section of its marginal cost curve that lies above its average variable cost curve

6. The long-run supply curve of a decreasing-cost industry is:

a. upward sloping

b. horizontal

c. downward sloping

d. vertical

7. A monopolist is so powerful that:

a. it cannot be regulated

b. it can control both price and output

c. both a and b

d. neither a nor b.

8. Ownership or control of essential raw materials can lead to:

a. price wars
b. the formation of monopoly
c. a monopoly losing its power
d. none of the above

9. The demand curve of a monopolist is:

a. highly elastic
b. inelastic
c. is the same as its marginal revenue curve
d. none of the above

10. Monopolists can exist in the long run because:

a. there are barriers to entry into the industry

b. they do not produce at the point where marginal revenue equals marginal cost

c. the long run is defined as a situation in which competition does not exist

d. they minimize cost rather than maximize profits

11. At its present level of output, a monopolist finds that its marginal revenue is greater than its marginal cost. To maximize profits, the monopolist should:

a. reduce price and leave output unchanged

b. increase price and leave output unchanged

c. continue to operate at current price and output levels

d. reduce price and increase output

12. The monopolist seeking to maximize profits will operate where its demand curve is:

a. inelastic
b. elastic
c. unitary elastic
d. perfectly elastic

13. Which of the following can be used to regulate a monopoly?

a. marginal-cost pricing

b. average-cost pricing

c. minimum average-cost pricing

d. all of the above

14. Successful advertising by a firm in monopolistic competition will:

a. shift the firm's demand curve to the right
b. shift the firm's demand curve to the left
c. make the firm's demand curve more elastic or less inelastic
d. cause kinks in the marginal revenue curve

15. In long-run equilibrium, a firm in monopolistic competition will:

a. earn positive economic profits

b. operate at the minimum point of its average cost curve

c. earn zero economic profit

d. operate where marginal cost equals average revenue

16. The excess capacity theorem relates to the fact that a profit-maximizing monopolistic competitor will produce:

a. an output level where long-run average cost (LRAC) equals zero

b. an output level less than the level that minimizes LRAC

d. its output with excess capacity no matter what output level is chosen

d. none of the above

17. An industry with only two firms is called:

a. a double monopoly

b. a duopoly

c. a cartel

d. none of the above

18. The model of the kinked demand curve applies to:

a. all monopolies
b. oligopoly
c. pure competition
d. all of the above

19. Which of the following is a problem typically faced by a *perfect* cartel?:

a. The tendency for individual members to cheat

b. The problem of deciding how production quotas should be set

c. The problem of deciding how profits should be distributed among members

d. All of the above

20. Nash equilibrium is:

a. a fake equilibrium that cannot be sustained

b. an equilibrium that can be achieved only by purely competitive firms

c. an equilibrium that can be achieved only by monopolies

d. none of the above

21. Oligopoly can be beneficial because it can lead to:

a. perfectly competitive behaviour

b. marginal-cost pricing

c. lower prices resulting from economies of scale

d. all of the above

PART 3. PROBLEMS AND EXERCISES (5 MARKS)

22. Answer the following questions on the basis of the following diagram. The firm's objective is to maximize profits

a. What output should the firm produce?

b. What price should it charge?

c. What price-quantity adjustment should the firm make following a $2 increase in marginal cost (MC)?

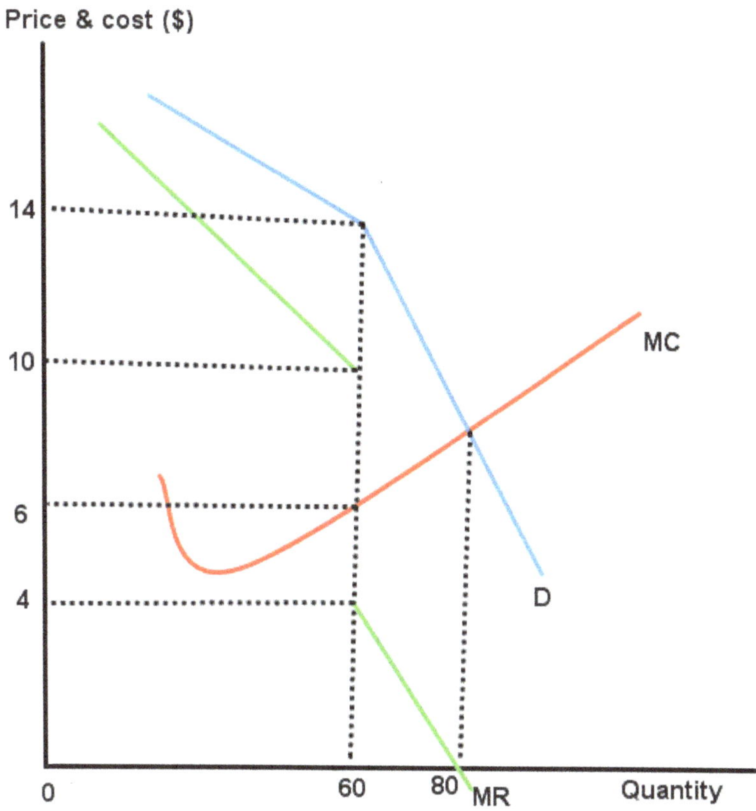

PART 4. ESSAY (5 MARKS)

23. What is a cartel? Give a real-world example of a cartel. What are some of the problems faced by cartels?

ANSWERS

Scenario 1: Hiring an Economist

Companies are increasingly recognizing the importance of economists to the success of their businesses; hence, they are hiring economists either as paid employees or as consultants. At LVC, an economist could perform a variety of functions that could help the company to achieve its objectives. Here are a few ways that having an economist on board could help.

Pricing

The prices that LVC charges for its products will determine the level of its profits. Economists study markets and can therefore help the company to price its products so that it earns maximum profits. It may be necessary for LVC to change its prices from time to time, depending on circumstances. Having an economist on staff would help the company to determine the effects of price changes on its profitability.

Estimating future demand

It is of vital importance for a company to be able to forecast demand for its products. Decisions made under conditions of certainty are likely to be superior to those made under uncertainty. Demand forecasting greatly reduces the amount of uncertainty in the decision-making process. Economists are experts in demand forecasting. The company will be able to properly plan its production levels, determine its requirement for raw materials, and eliminate waste.

Policy impact

Government policies affect the economic environment within which companies operate and may affect companies directly. An economist could carefully analyze the impact of public policy and provide LVC with the relevant information so that it can appropriately respond to such policies.

Scenario 2: What exactly do Economists do?

Job description for an economist

Duties and responsibilities

The economist:

1. Provides relevant data by conducting research on economic issues
2. Determines trends by analyzing and interpreting data
3. Contributes to good decision-making by advising executives
4. Reports research findings by preparing reports, tables, and graphs
5. Solves economic problems by using appropriate economic models
6. Predicts economic outcomes by using statistical and econometric models
7. Increases overall effectiveness by collaborating with specialists from other disciplines.

Job requirements and skills

The economist should have a minimum of a master's degree in economics. He or she should possess excellent communication (written and oral) skills. The ability to work as a team member is a necessity.

Scenario 3: Economic Growth—A Controversial Issue? Applying Economic Reasoning

The benefits of economic growth are undeniable and are hardly in dispute. The controversial issue is whether or not the pursuit of more economic growth is desirable. The economic way of thinking can be applied to this situation so that a valid conclusion can be reached. As noted in the scenario, there are benefits (enumerated by the supporters of more growth) and there are costs (enumerated by the detractors of more growth). Economists make decisions at the margin. In considering a course of action, they weigh the additional benefits against the additional costs. If the extra benefits outweigh the extra costs of pursuing the course of action, then the action should be taken. Otherwise, the course of action should not be taken. The relevant question here is whether or not more economic growth should be pursued.

The following diagram will help to illustrate the decision-making process.

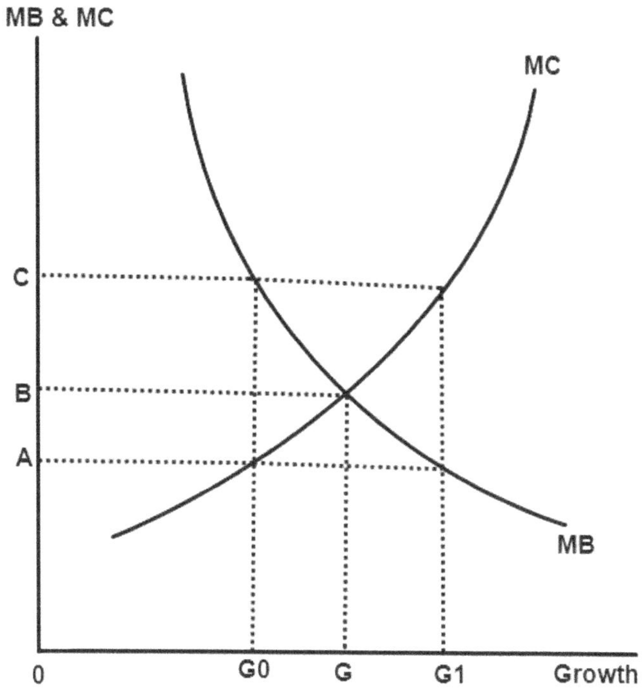

MB and MC are marginal benefits and marginal cost curves respectively. If the level of economic growth in Econoville is G0, then the additional benefit of pursuing further growth, C, exceeds the additional cost, A; therefore, additional growth should be pursued. On the other hand, if the level of growth is G1, the extra benefit of pursuing more growth, A, is less than the additional cost, C; therefore growth should be curtailed. At an economic growth of G, the marginal benefit is just equal to the marginal cost at B. This is the optimum amount of economic growth that Econoville should pursue.

Scenario 4: Economics, a Science? Never!

Dear Mr. Freeman,

I read your article about economics and I was appalled at your obvious ignorance of the subject. It is obvious that you have never studied economics, and if you did, then it has definitely escaped you. Let me enlighten you, Sir. In order to qualify as a science, a field of study must follow a certain procedure which is called the scientific approach. It involves data collection, observation and measurement; the formulation of testable hypotheses; experimentation; and verification. This is the essence of science and this is how economists study the economy. So you see, Mr. Freeman, economics does not claim to be a science; it *is* a science in every sense of the word.

Scenario 5: Why Don't They Listen? Economists as Advisers

It is true that the recommendations of economic advisers are not always followed. Leaders often surround themselves with advisers in a variety of areas—political, communications, legal, etc. When the economic advisers report their recommendations, it is not that the Prime Minister and other leaders do not listen, but before they make a decision, they consider inputs from other advisers. It is not only the economic effects with which they are concerned. How will certain powerful interest groups react to the policy? Will the leader's support base be weakened by the policy? Will the policy be seen generally as the right thing to do? Leaders hear and weigh all these and other considerations before deciding what course of action to take. So for these reasons, although the economic advisers might do an excellent job in providing valuable input, their advice might not be followed.

Scenario 6: Economists at the Picnic. Disagreement among Economists

The issue between Dan and Paul on the tax matter is obviously normative in nature. They hold different opinions as to whether or not the tax should be imposed on cigarettes. Such differences in values and opinions are a major cause of disagreement among economists, and it is clearly reflected in the exchange between Dan and Paul. The issue regarding the extent to which a fall in the rate of interest affects the level of investment is a positive issue, yet Paul and Jim disagree. In this case, they disagree over the magnitude of the change. This type of disagreement may be prolonged because of the lack of adequate empirical data.

Scenario 7: A Land Flowing with Milk and Honey. Any Scarcity Here?

a. Miss Green and Mr. Brown seem to be looking at the vast array of resources and are puzzled by the notion of scarcity as applied to Jorobel. In an absolute sense, the country may be flowing with milk and honey. Abundance everywhere. The concept of scarcity that they must have had in mind is absolute scarcity.

b. Even in Jorobel, with its abundance of valuable resources, scarcity still exists. There would not be sufficient resources to enable Jorobel to produce all the goods and services that would be necessary to satisfy all the wants of all its citizens. Thus relative scarcity or economic scarcity exists even in Jorobel. Miss Green and Mr. Brown both face scarcity. In order to attend the party, they must sacrifice some other activity—maybe a quiet evening at home with their families.

Scenario 8: The Cost of Attending University May Be More Than You Think

    a. An extremely important cost item that is missing from the calculation of John's total cost of attending university is the income that he could have earned instead of attending university. Economists refer to this type of cost as *opportunity cost*.

    b. The total cost to John of attending university is all the cost items listed in the table plus the opportunity cost. That is $29,500 + $30,000 = $59,500.

    c. If John was unemployed before he decided to attend university, then the opportunity of his attending university would be zero. Therefore his cost would be $29,500. One further consideration is the $6,500 that he pays for the room. This figure might have to be adjusted if John would live at home had he not decided to attend university.

Scenario 9: Enrolment Planning. Anything to do with Opportunity Cost?

At first glance, it would seem that the university administrator's view is correct. After all, attending university is costly—tuition fees, possible room and board, books, transportation, etc. are just some of the expenses involved. In a period of high unemployment, income tends to fall, so the ability to pay tuition fees tends to be less, resulting in a decrease in enrolment. However, when one considers the full cost of attending university, one must look not only at the direct expenses. The biggest cost is often the opportunity cost—the income the students could have earned instead of going to university. In deciding to attend university, one should consider the full cost of doing so. Other things being equal, the higher the cost of attending university, the lower the enrolment will be. During a period of high unemployment, the full cost of attending university is relatively low because the prospects of finding employment are low. The opportunity cost is practically zero so one should expect enrolment to increase. The consultant's view is correct, so those additional classrooms should be prepared.

Scenario 10: Calculating Real Profit. The Economist's Approach

The Income Statement provided for Bread of Life Bakery and Café shows that the bakery made a net profit of $290,500. Violet had good reason to smile when she looked at the bottom line. If she had accepted the position of manager of the competing bakery, she would have earned only $60,000 as salary which is significantly less than her earning from her bakery. But the figures in the Income Statement don't tell the whole story.

The Income Statement presented for Bread of Life has omitted a major cost item—the salary of $60,000 that Violet could have earned as manager of the competing bakery. Economists refer to this type of cost as *opportunity cost*. Adding this cost to the $309,500 recorded as operating expenses brings the true cost of operating the business to $369,500. So in reality then, it turns out that Violet's earnings, from an economic perspective, is $600,000 − 369,500 = $230,500. She has earned (230,500 − 60,000 = $170,000 more than she would have earned as manager of the competing bakery.

Scenario 11: Presentation for the Park. Explain It with Production Possibilities Curves

Series of Graphs for the Director of Parks and Recreation

The following series of production-possibility graphs will suffice.

a. The following graph shows that with its given budget, the Department of Parks and Recreation can provide many combinations of parking spaces and playground equipment. If the department is operating at point A, it can get more playground equipment by moving to point B, but that would entail giving up some parking spaces.

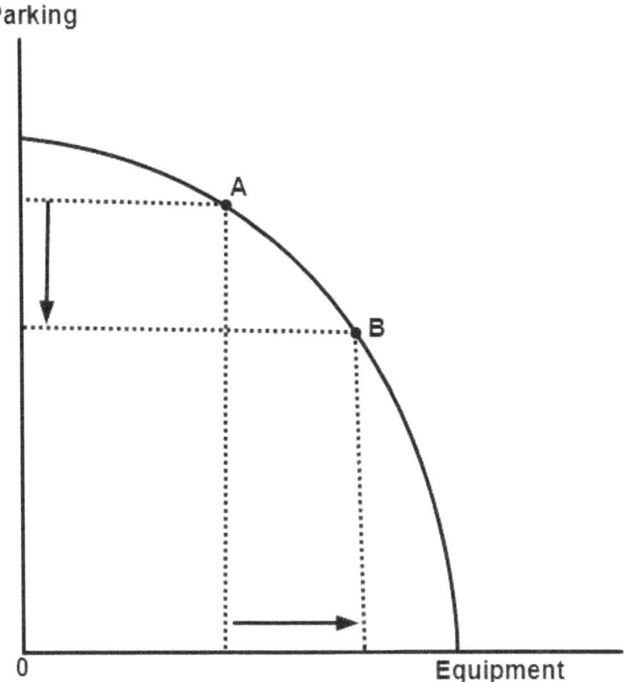

b. The production-possibility curve (PPC) will shift out as shown below. The ability to increase parking spaces will rise while the ability to provide more playground equipment will be unaffected. The shift in the PPC is non-parallel.

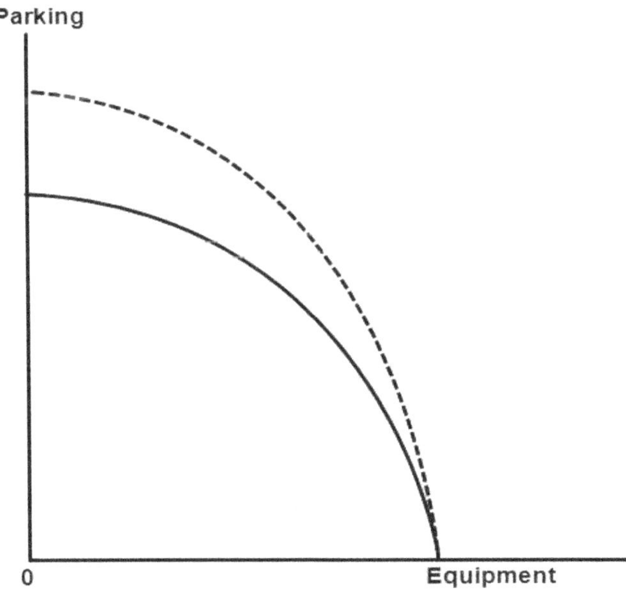

c. The increase in demand for parking spaces will have no effect on the Department's ability to provide parking spaces or playground equipment; hence the department's PPC will not be affected. As shown in the diagram below, the curve does not shift.

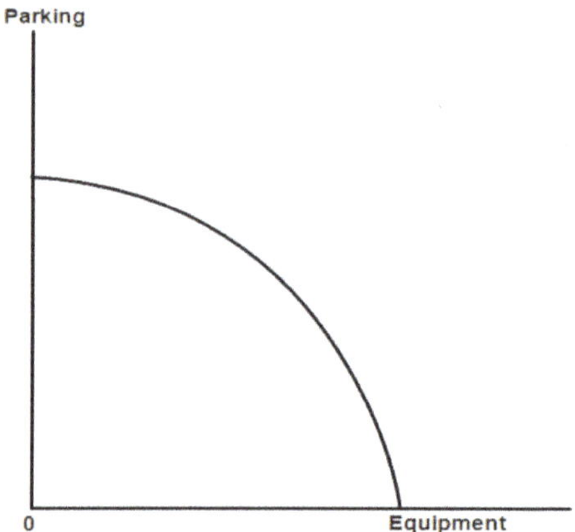

d. An increase in the budget for the Department of Parks and Recreation means that the department will be able to provide both more playground equipment *and* more parking spaces. As shown in the following diagram, the PPC will shift outward.

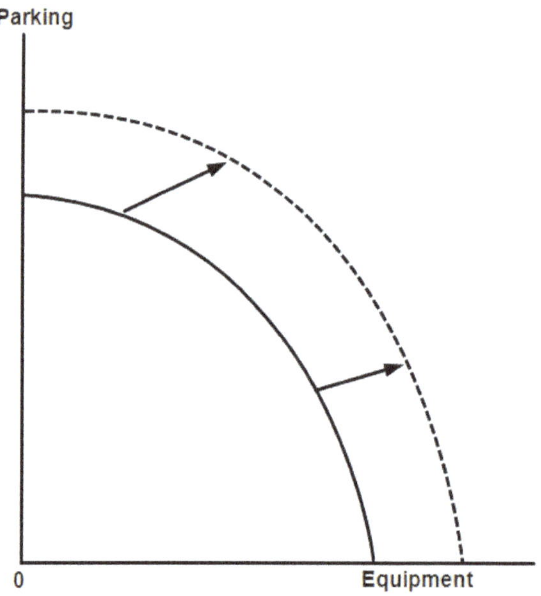

Scenario 12: Not a Drum was heard for the Free Market System

The free market system is not a perfect system, and some of the claims against it are true, but the system does have very important advantages. In a market-oriented economic system, individuals enjoy freedom of choice. Individuals and groups are free to own resources and to use them to advance their own self-interest, thus the system provides incentives for people to pursue their economic objectives and improve their economic well-being as they perceive them. Under a free market economic system, every individual has an opportunity to use his or her talents and resources for his or her own benefit.

Under the free market economic system, the goods and services that consumers want are produced without any deliberate coordinated decision-making. The system works automatically for the most part and is therefore relatively efficient. In such a system, there is no need to make special arrangements with a grocery store to provide you with milk today. If you wanted to, you could go confidently to the grocery store knowing that you could buy the milk you wanted. Under this system, you don't have to make any arrangements with the university cafeteria for your two eggs, toast, coffee, and orange juice on any particular morning, yet you are quite confident that you will be able to obtain breakfast any morning. The system works in such a way that it does not require a great deal of coordination for a market-oriented economy to produce the goods and services that consumers want to buy.

Scenario 13: What is the Question? The Free Market Answers

O.K., Eugene. The "what" problem is what to produce? The economy faces scarcity of resources so it cannot produce all the goods and services that are required to satisfy all human wants. If it produces more cars, it must produce fewer classrooms. Now listen carefully because this is the part that you don't understand. In a free enterprise system, firms engage in production because they hope to make a profit by selling the product at a price that exceeds the cost of production. It follows then, that firms will produce what consumers want to buy. Consumers express their wants by their behavior in the market. Firms respond by producing those goods and services that receive the highest number of dollar votes. Suppose a manufacturing company decides to produce a certain product called *cuties* and then finds out that consumers are unwilling to spend their money on that particular product. The firm will soon discover that the production of *cuties* is not profitable and will put its resources into some other venture. By their decision not to purchase *cuties*, consumers have communicated effectively to the manufacturing company that they do not want *cuties* produced. The free enterprise economic system thus decides "what" to produce.

Scenario 14: Search and You will Find the Circular Flow Model

The diagram is called a *circular flow model*, and we studied it in class just two days ago. Resources (those are the things like labour and land that are used to produce goods and services) flow from the households (people like you and me and our parents and friends) to the factor market. In this market, households sell their resources to firms in exchange for money. You will notice a flow of resources from the factor market to the firms and a flow of money from the factor market to the households.

Now, the firms have the resources and the households have money which is the income they receive from selling their resources. The firms use the resources to produce goods and services (products) that they sell to households in the product market. Notice the flow of goods and services from the firms to the product market and the flow of money from the households to the product market. After the exchange takes place, there is a flow of goods and services (products) from the product market to the households and a flow of money from the product market to the firms.

Scenario 15: Fluctuations in Gas Prices. Demand and Supply Can Explain Them

This document illustrates that fluctuations in gas prices may be due to factors other than price-fixing and collusion by oil companies. Specifically, this analysis shows that the market forces of demand and supply can explain the fluctuations observed in gas prices over the past three years. Four cases are considered.

1. *An increase in demand:* During holidays, the demand for gasoline tends to increase as motorists tend to travel longer distances. In the following graph, the demand curve for gasoline shifts to the right and the equilibrium price rises from P to P1 as shown in the diagram.

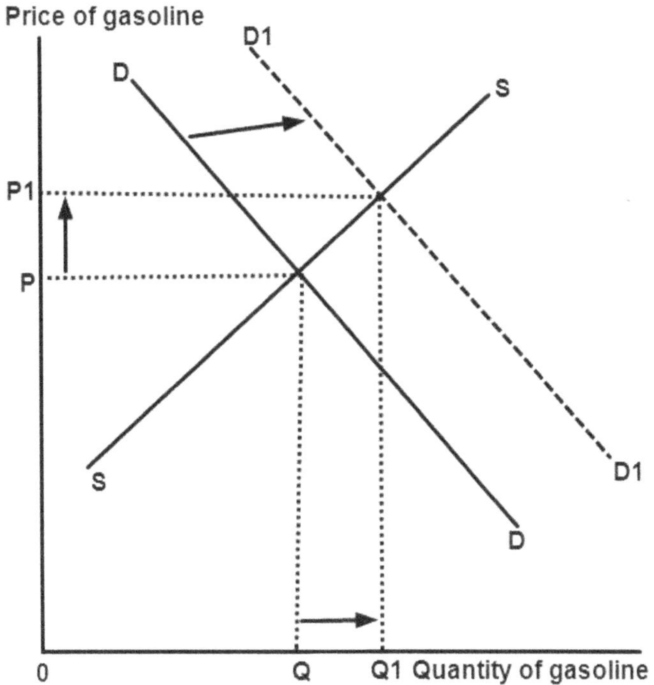

2. *A decrease in demand:* During the winter season and on very cold days, the demand for gasoline tends to decrease as travellers tend to restrict their movements because of the cold. As a result, the demand curve shifts to the left from DD to D0D0, and the price rises falls from P to P0 as shown.

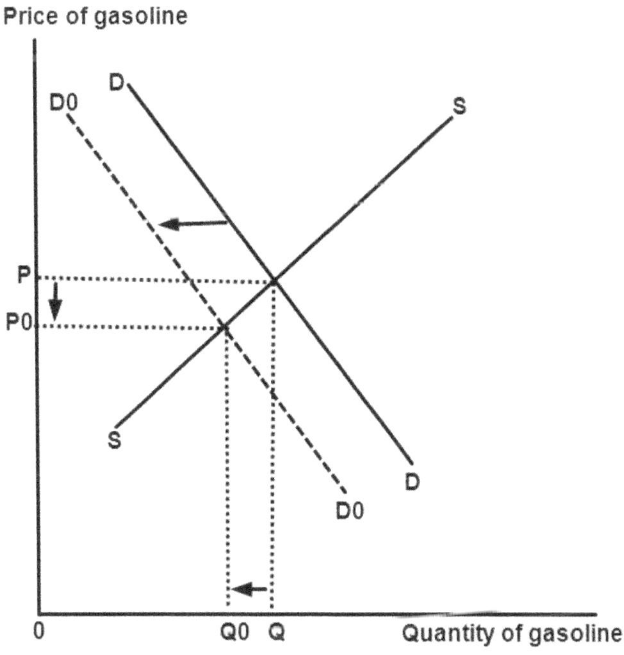

3. *An increase in supply:* Faster extraction of oil increases the supply of gasoline. This causes the supply curve to shift to the right from SS to S1S1 as shown in the diagram, and the price falls from P to P0.

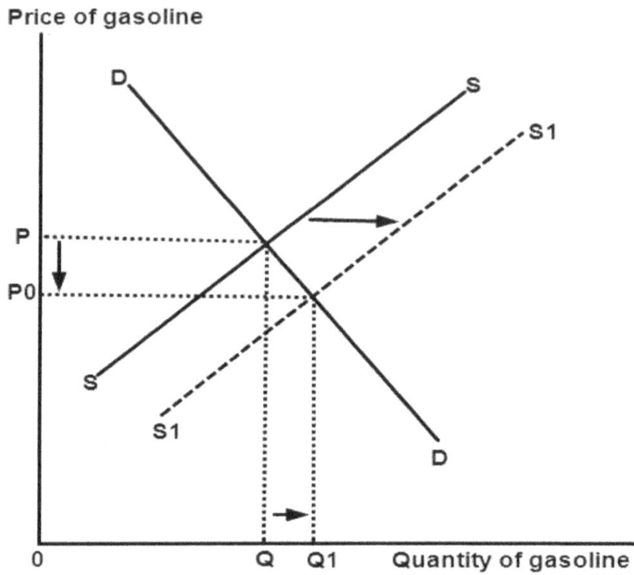

1. *A decrease in supply:* An accidental oilfield fire will reduce the supply of oil and hence the supply of gasoline. As seen in the graph below, the supply curve shifts to the left and the price rises.

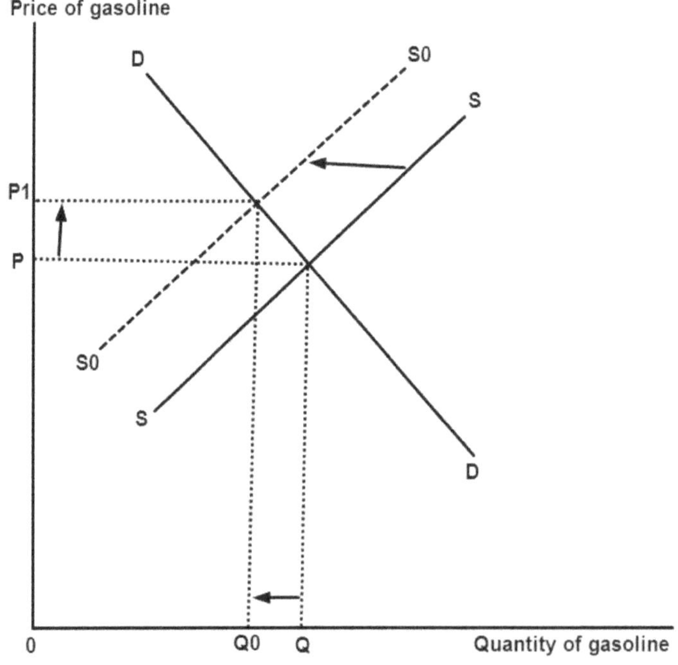

Scenario 16: Review of Residence Pricing Policy at Best Business University

At a price of $2,500 per semester, the quantity of rooms demanded is 115; but BBU can accommodate only 105 students. Thus, BBU's current pricing policy results in a shortage of rooms in its dormitories. The university is charging a price that is too low. A higher price would lower the quantity of rooms demanded and thus get rid of or reduce the shortage. The demand schedule shows that the quantity of rooms demanded and the quantity supplied are equal at 105 rooms, when the rate is $2,700/semester. Thus to clear the market (achieve equilibrium), BBU should increase its rate to $2,700. This increase in the price of its rooms will have no effect on the *demand* for accommodation, but the *quantity demanded* will fall. Accommodation at neighbouring residences must be seen as substitutes for rooms at BBU. Therefore, if neighbouring residences raise their rates, students will switch to the now relatively cheaper rooms at BBU. One would expect the demand for rooms at BBU's dormitories to increase.

Price per room/ semester ($)	Quantity of rooms demanded/ semester
2,800	100
2,700	105
2,600	110
2,500	115
2,400	120
2,300	125
2,200	130

Scenario 17: Arise and Shine: The Market for Coffee

On the basis of the demand schedule for coffee at Bread of Life Bakery and Café, Violet's intention to charge a price of $4 per package of coffee will not achieve her objective of selling her entire stock and leaving customers not wanting more or less. At that price, she will sell only 1,000 packages, leaving a surplus of 1,000 packages. To accomplish her objective, Violet will have to lower the price to $3.00. At this price, customers will be willing and able to buy the entire stock of 2,000 packages.

The market will be in equilibrium. A similar product at Daily Bread would be considered a substitute for coffee from Bread of Life Bakery and Café. If Daily Bread increases the price of its coffee, customers will switch to Bread of Life so the demand for coffee from Bread of Life will increase. On the other hand, if Daily Bread reduces its price, the demand for the product from Bread of Life will fall as customers switch from Bread of Life to Daily Bread whose price would now be cheaper.

Scenario 18: The Politics and Economics of Minimum Wage Legislation

In many (if not most) jurisdictions, minimum wage legislation is a fact of life. The stated purpose of such legislation is to ensure that workers earn a decent wage and that employers do not take unfair advantage of employees. This document analyzes the economic effects of minimum wage legislation.

The following graph of the labour market will help to illustrate the argument. The demand curve for labour is **DL** and the supply curve is **SL**. The market equilibrium wage rate is determined by the intersection of the demand and supply curves. This equilibrium wage rate is indicated by **We**. At this wage rate, the quantity of labour demanded is **L** and the quantity supplied is also **L**. There is no surplus or shortage of workers.

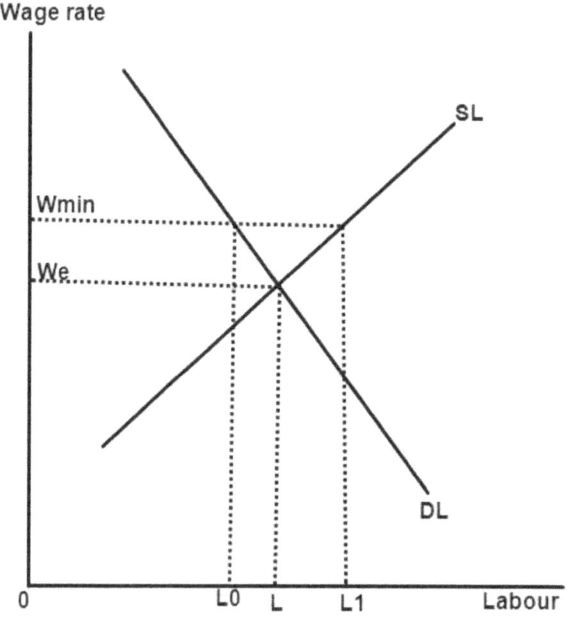

If the minimum wage is set below the market equilibrium of **We**, it will have no effect. The equilibrium wage rate will prevail. However, if the minimum wage is set above the market equilibrium wage, such as **Wmin** in the diagram, the number of workers that will be hired by employers will be **L0**, while the number of workers seeking employment will be **L1**. Thus, the number of workers who will not be hired is (**L1 − L0**). This represents unemployment that it due to the minimum wage legislation.

Scenario 19: Rent Control to the Rescue? A Better Way?

a. Let us consider the market for rental units. The demand for rental units is shown by the curve DD in the diagram, and the supply is shown by the curve SS. The market equilibrium rent is $700 per month and at that price, 1,700 units are demanded (rented) and supplied. In other words, the market clears at that price.

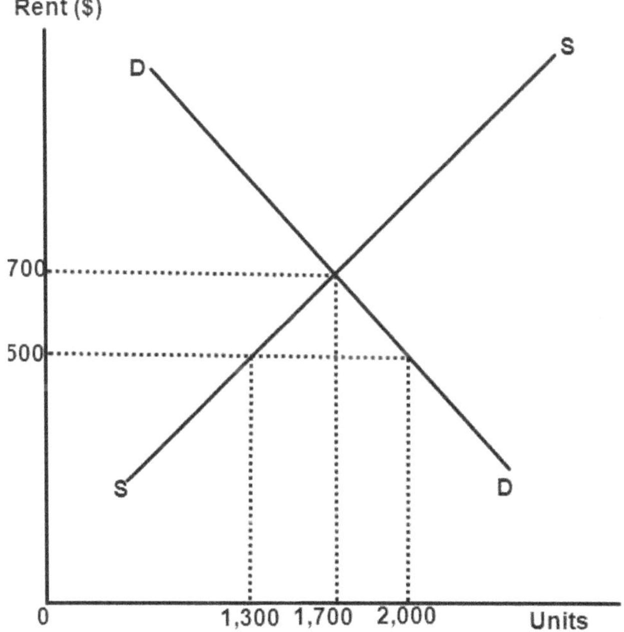

Now, suppose the Rent Control Board decides to limit rent to $500 per month. At this price, the quantity demanded jumps to 2,000 units while the quantity supplied falls to 1,300 units. The action of the Rent Control Board has created a shortage of rental units of (2,000 − 1,300) = 700. At the administered price of $500 a month, landlords may not have any incentives to maintain their buildings. Needed repairs are left undone, and the buildings begin to deteriorate—the development of slums.

c. If the city considers rent to be too high at $700 per month, one alternative to rent control would be to provide incentives such as tax breaks to developers to increase the supply of rental units. Also, the city could enter the housing market and build affordable rental units. Such measures would shift the supply curve to the right and reduce the rent.

Scenario 20: Farmers on the Move. Quotas and All That

a. Significant increases in the productivity of farmers over the years have increased the supply of farm products, thus lowering their prices. As the prices of farm products fall, the quantity demanded does not increase much. There is only so much food that people can eat. The incomes of farmers therefore do not increase significantly. When incomes in the society increase, the demand for most goods and services also increases. However, the increase in demand for farm products does not keep pace with the increase in demand for other goods and services, so farmers do not benefit as much as the rest of society.

b. The imposition of a quota on farm products raises the prices of farm products. It is possible for this increase in the prices of farm products to improve the well-being of farmers. The following diagram of the market for farm products will help to illustrate the idea.

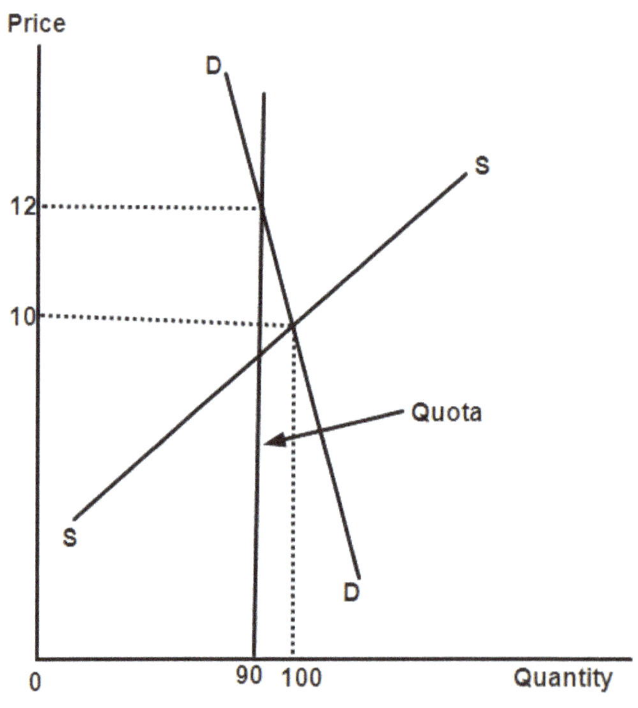

The demand and supply for farm products is shown by DD and SS respectively. The steepness of the DD curve implies that changes in the prices of farm products do not meaningfully affect the quantity demanded. The equilibrium price is $10 and the equilibrium quantity is 100. Farm income is therefore ($10 × 100) = $1,000.

Now, suppose the quota is set at 90, which is 10% less than the equilibrium quantity of 100. If the price rises by 20% as a result of the fall in supply, the price will rise from $10 to $12. Farm income will now be ($12 × 90) = $1,080. In this case, the quota increases farm income by $80.

Scenario 21: Here Comes Professor Noce. Beware of False Demand and Supply Doctrines

There are several errors and misunderstandings in the professor's responses. First, it should be noted that an increase in the demand for laptops cannot be the result of a fall in their prices. A fall in the price of laptop computers will lead to an increase in the quantity of laptop computers demanded, not to an increase in demand. Contrary to Professor Noce's assertion, the law of demand states that if the price of an item falls, other things being equal, the quantity demanded will rise, and vice versa.

Second, when asked what happens to price when demand increases, the professor declared that he was not sure. His explanation was that when demand increases, price rises, and when price rises, demand falls. The fall in demand will lower the price. So the effect of an increase in demand on price is ambiguous. The professor is wrong. When demand increases, other things being equal, price will rise. When price rises, the quantity demanded (not demand) falls. The professor confused demand and quantity demanded.

Third, the professor's response to the question regarding complementary goods is hilarious. Simply stated, complementary goods are goods that are used together. Computers and USB flash drives are complementary goods; so are automobiles and tires, and chalk and chalk board.

Finally, supply and demand are related but certainly not in the sense that the professor explains it. Actually, when demand increases, nothing happens to supply as a result, but the quantity supplied does increase; and when supply increases, nothing happens to demand as a result, but the quantity supplied does increase.

Scenario 22: Sally's Dilemma—Math to the Rescue

The demand for and supply of Sally's bags is as follows:

$$Qd = 130 - 3P$$

$$Qs = 100$$

For the market (in this case Sally's) to clear, the quantity of bags demanded must be equal to the quantity supplied. Therefore,

$$130 - 3P = 100$$

$$-3P = -30$$

$$P = 10$$

Sally should charge **$10** for her bags.

Now, if the demand for her bags increases by 15, the demand equation will become

$Qd = (130 + 15) - 3P$, and the supply equation will remain unchanged at $Qs = 100$

For the market to clear (neither a shortage nor a shortage), the quantity demanded and the quantity supplied must be equal. Thus:

$$(130 + 15) - 3P = 100$$

$$145 - 3P = 100$$

$$-3P = -45$$

$$P = 15$$

Sally should increase the price of her bags from $10 to **$15**.

Scenario 23: Raising Revenue by Raising Price. Good Advice?

Sally's explanation is erroneous and simplistic. Raising and lowering revenue is not just a matter of simply raising and lowering price. Elasticity is an important part of the equation. If demand is elastic, lowering price will cause quantity demanded to rise proportionately more than the fall in price. Thus, total revenue will increase. If demand in inelastic, lowering the price will cause quantity demanded to rise proportionately less than the fall in price. Thus total revenue will fall.

Scenario 24: Elasticity and Slope—A Matter of Semantics: Professor Noce Lectures

Professor Noce!!! A matter of semantics? Not at all. Although slope and elasticity are closely related, they are not identical. The difference can be easily demonstrated. The elasticity along a linear demand curve varies from point to point, but the slope is constant. Also, the slope of a linear demand curve is $\Delta P/\Delta Q$ while the elasticity is $\Delta Q/\Delta P \times P/Q$. The difference is obvious.

Scenario 25: Either There is a Response or no Response to a Change in Price. Don't be Confused.

John would probably say something like this: Elasticity is a measure of responsiveness, but it focuses on *degrees* of responsiveness. It compares the percentage change in quantity with the percentage change in prices. Degrees of elasticity can be seen as a spectrum from perfectly inelastic at one end to perfectly elastic at the other.

Scenario 26: Jorobel Revisited. Computing Total Revenue and Price Elasticity

Table 1 Data for the Demand for Wallets in Jorobel

Price ($)	Quantity Bought (000)	Total Revenue ($000)	Elasticity Coefficient
10	100	1,000	
			2.0
9	120	1,080	
			1.5
8	140	1,120	
			1.14
7	160	1,120	
			0.88
6	180	1,080	
			0.67
5	200	1,000	

a. See table above

b. See table above

c. When demand is elastic, a fall in price causes total revenue to increase. When demand is inelastic, a fall in price causes total revenue to decrease.

Scenario 27: What items to tax?

Ideally, one would tax items with inelastic demands. These include:

1. Gasoline
2. Baby clothes
3. Matches
4. Cigarettes
5. Salt
6. Chocolate
7. Toilet paper
8. Prescribed medication
9. Textbook for a university course
10. Coffee

Scenario 28: The True Meaning of Utility

Sarah's thoughts are erroneous. She equates utility with usefulness. In fact, in economics, utility is satisfaction.

Scenario 29: The Difference between Total Utility and Marginal Utility. Just a Dream?

The definitions given by the professor in Sabrina's dream are erroneous. Total utility is the total (not maximum) satisfaction derived from consuming an item. Marginal utility, on the other hand, is the extra satisfaction given by an additional unit of an item.

Scenario 30: What are they doing? Maximizing what?

Economists assume that all those shoppers at the mall have one objective, and that is to maximize their satisfaction subject to their budget constraint.

Scenario 31: The *Real* Crux of the Matter. Don't Forget the Budget

If the consumer had unlimited funds, then he or she would try to attain the highest indifference curve because that would give maximum satisfaction. The reality, however, is that the consumer is constrained by his or her budget. To be in equilibrium, the consumer must be on the highest indifference curve *consistent with his or her budget line.*

Scenario 32: Will the Real Indifference Curve Please Stand Up?

Indifference curves have three properties:

1. They are downward-sloping
2. They are convex
3. They are non-intersecting

Scenario 33: How to allocate budget to maximize satisfaction. Can they really do that?

The consumer will be in equilibrium when the budget is distributed in such a way that MUA/PA = MUB/PB. MUA/PA = MUB/PB = 8 when the consumer buys 3 units of A for $6, and 2 units of B for $6, making a total of $12. See table below.

Quantity of A	MUA	MUA/PA	Quantity of B	MUB	MUB/PB
1	16	8	1	21	7
2	18	9	2	24	8
3	16	8	3	18	6
4	14	7	4	15	5
5	10	5	5	12	4
6	6	3	6	6	2
7	2	1	7	3	1

Scenario 34: Not the Boston Tea Party; An important business decision

Mr. Anderson's problem seems to be a decline in patronage for his shop. The affluent society in which is located may not be interested in his second-hand goods. Mr. Anderson might respond to this situation by changing his product offering from used goods to new goods. Alternatively, he might consider moving his shop from its present location to a low-income area where there may be a greater demand for his goods.

Scenario 35: Conflict of interest? Profits or revenue?

Profit maximization and revenue maximization may not be consistent objectives. The manager wants to sell as much as possible to earn revenue and may be less inclined to control cost than is the owner, whose objective is to maximize profits. For example, lowering the price of the product may increase revenue, but it may also reduce profits.

Scenario 36: Decisions! Decisions! Decisions! Which method to use?

The choice between methods 1 and 2 will be made on the basis of their relative economic efficiency. Using method 1, the cost of the inputs is (10 × $5) + (6 × $6) = $86. The value of the output is (24 × $10) = $240. Therefore, the economic efficiency ratio is 240 ÷ 86 = 2.79. Using method 2, the cost of the inputs is (15 ×$5) + (2 × $6) = $87. The value of the output is (25 × $10) = $250. Therefore, the economic efficiency ratio is 250 ÷ 87 = 2.87. Method 2 should be chosen, because it is more economically efficient.

Scenario 37: Total product, average product, and marginal product. Show me in pictures.

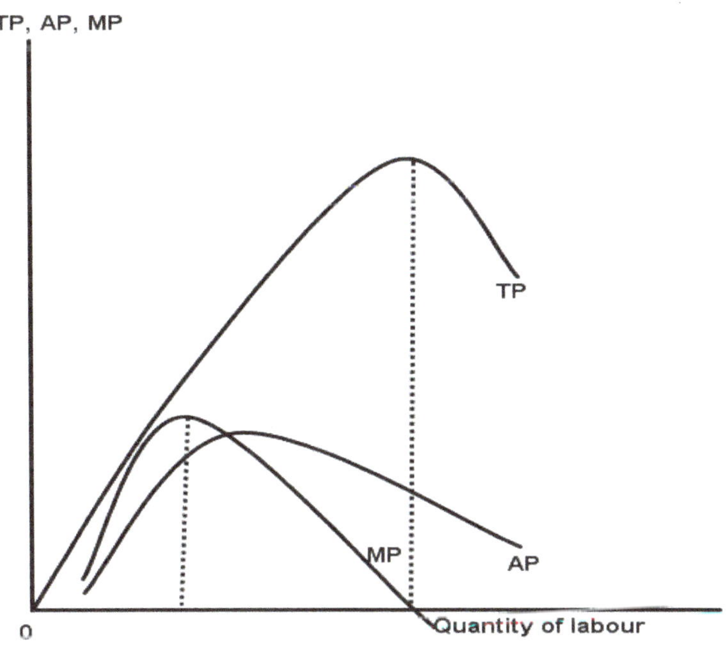

Scenario 38: Professor Charl A. Tan lectures on technology and production

Modern technology causes the user to produce the same quantity of output with fewer inputs, or a greater quantity of output with the same inputs. The following diagram illustrates the effect of modern technology on total production. TP is the original total product curve. Modern technology shifts the curve up to TP1.

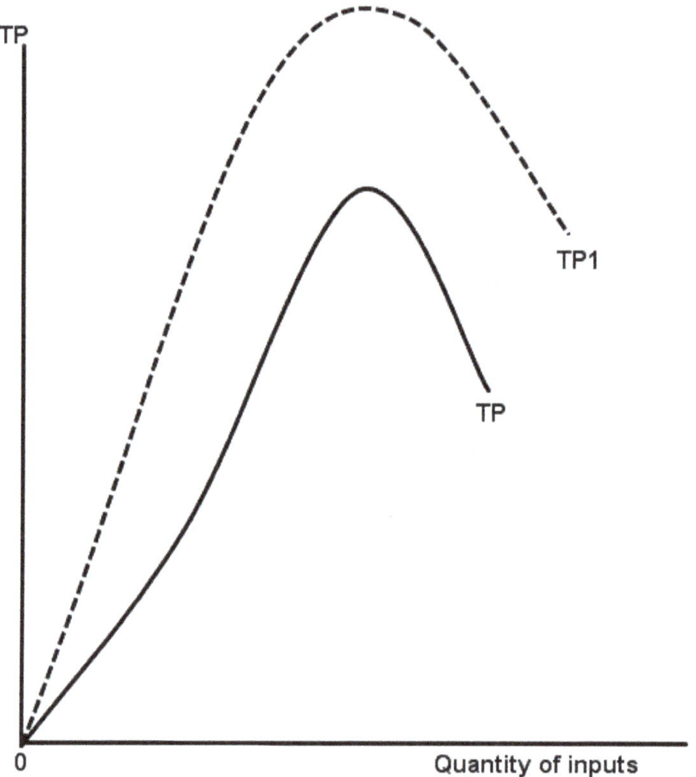

Scenario 39: Study Group in Economics: Sharing the Work on the Principle of Substitution

Here is a splendid opportunity to apply the principle of substitution. As the cost of capital (machines) falls, the last dollar spent on capital increases productivity more than if that dollar were spent on labour. Thus, to minimize cost, the enterprise should by more capital and less labour.

Scenario 40: Professor Noce Comments on the Law of Diminishing Returns

The good professor is wrong on all counts.

1. Contrary to Professor Noce, the law of diminishing returns applies to the short run because it talks about a fixed factor.
2. The law does not apply only to agriculture. It applies to any production process in which there is a fixed factor.
3. Diminishing returns set in after the *marginal* product has reached its maximum.

Scenario 41: You Had a Dream—A Conference of Economists

1. *Reflections:* 1. Judging from the attendance, there seems to be a great deal of interest in economics.
2. Developments in microeconomics are due to the contributions of a wide variety of economists.
3. We can better appreciate current economic principles by knowing the people who contributed to their development.
4. It is interesting to note that many people know and appreciate the economists who made significant contributions to the field of economics.

Scenario 42: This train is bound for Salem and Plymouth. Special production function

On the basis of the reference to Salem, Plymouth, production function, and Amherst College, it is safe to assume that the two men were Charles Cobb and Paul Douglas of the Cobb-Douglas production function fame.

Scenario 43: Keep an eye on those inventories. They are crucial in production planning

Inventories do "speak" to producers about the need to vary output to suit demand. Firms keep a certain amount of inventory to meet unanticipated changes in demand. If inventories rise above their intended or planned levels, then the firms' production levels are too high for the current level of demand. An unplanned accumulation of inventories is therefore a signal to producers to reduce their volume of output. The inventories are saying, "We are too much, cut production levels."

On the other hand, if inventories fall below their intended levels, then the firm's production levels are too low for the current level of demand. This situation would be a signal to the firms to increase their volume of output. The inventories are saying, "We are not enough, increase production levels." Unintended changes in inventories thus serve as a barometer that the firms may use to adjust their output to the appropriate level.

Scenario 44: To Accept or Not to Accept? That Is the Question

Carolyn has to account for all the resources used in her bakery. This includes the $15 000 she could have earned for her building. Her true situation then is:

Total revenue	$320 000
Total cost ($200 000 + 15 000)	$215 000
Total profits	$105 000

She could earn a salary of $120 000 which is more than the $105 000 she earns from her bakery. Other things being equal, she should accept the offer.

Scenario 45: Algebra Can Help Us to get from Total to Average, even when talking about cost

Let us begin with the equation for total cost. TC = TFC + TVC, where TC is total cost, TFC is total fixed cost, and TVC is total variable cost. If we divide each term in the equation by quantity (Q), we obtain

TC/Q = TFC/Q + TVC/Q

which is ATC = AFC + AVC

Yes, it's as easy as the professor claimed.

Scenario 46: Professor Ecnud's Notes on Cost Curves

1. Not all unit cost curves are U-shaped. The average fixed cost curve declines continuously.
2. The minimum point of the average total cost curve occurs at a higher level of output than that of the average variable cost curve
3. The average fixed cost curve does not have a minimum point
4. The average total cost curve and the average variable cost curve come closer and closer together as output increases

Scenario 47: A Parade of "Marginals". Play the Game

The following are marginal concepts encountered in microeconomics:

Marginal benefit The extra benefit derived from carrying out an additional unit of an activity

Marginal cost The extra cost of producing one additional unit of output

Marginal physical product The extra output produced by employing an additional unit of a variable factor

Marginal rate of substitution The rate at which one item can be traded for another without changing the consumer's level of satisfaction. It is the slope of the indifference curve

Marginal revenue The extra revenue obtained from selling ad additional unit of an item

Marginal utility The extra satisfaction derived from consuming an additional unit of an item

Scenario 48: Meeting at the Restaurant—Economies of Scale?

By centralizing its purchases, Food Sense can take advantage of huge quantity discounts that might not be available on smaller quantities to individual outlets. Also, by being a large-volume buyer, Food Sense might be able to exercise some strength in negotiations with its suppliers.

Scenario 49: Economic Concept Explains Panasonic's Product Offering

Panasonic's product offering is truly extensive. However, the products are all related to electronics. Economies of scope can likely fully explain Panasonic's product offering.

Scenario 50: Economies of Scope? Is there such a thing?

There is such a thing as economies of scope. It exists when the costs of producing different goods together are less than they would be if the goods were produced separately. When economies of scope exist, it is justifiable (even desirable) for firms to product multiple products together.

Scenario 51: Pure Competition? It's a Fantasy. It's Not Real

The firm in pure competition can sell as much as it wants to sell at the existing price. Advertising has a cost, but it bestows no benefit to the firm. It follows that if the firm is rational, it will not engage in competitive advertising. It will not incur a cost that has no benefits.

Scenario 52: An Economic Consultant to advise on Pricing Policy

In pure competition, firms are price-takers and quantity-adjusters. Each profit-seeking firm decides on the quantity to produce but has no control over the price. That being the case, a pricing policy is useless. It makes no sense to hire an economist for that purpose.

Scenario 53: To Advertise or not to advertise. Hard choice

This is not really a hard choice. Fashion Boutique can sell as much as it wants at the existing price. It has nothing to gain from advertising. It should reject the agent's offer.

Scenario 54: If it's not earning a profit, shut it down. That is Professor Charl A. Tan's motto

Professor Charl A. Tan must be a charlatan. This is the short run, and as long as the price is above the average variable cost, and marginal revenue equals marginal cost, the firm should not shut down. By continuing to operate, the firm is minimizing its losses.

Scenario 55: Tough decision at Loose Leaf

The situation is similar to the theoretical long-run equilibrium of a firm in pure competition. Mr. Brooks's resources, including his entrepreneurial skills, were earning as much as they could earn in the next best alternative use. That being the case, Mr. Brooks had no reason to leave the industry and made the right decision.

Scenario 56: Who knows the answer? Pareto optimality

Pareto optimality or Pareto efficiency is the condition that exists when it is impossible to make someone better off without making someone else worse off. The concept is named after the economist Vilfredo Pareto.

Scenario 57: Utterly confused. Is it useful?

The model of pure competition is often regarded as a kind of straw man. Although real-world examples of pure competition may be hard to find, the model is still useful. It serves as an ideal by which by which we can measure other market structures. We can, in fact, consider it a kind of measuring rod. Moreover, many of the prescriptions of the purely competitive model hold true even in situations where pure competition does not prevail.

Scenario 58: Protection available?

Tropical Pharmaceuticals can protect its product by obtaining a patent from the government. This patent will provide some measure of protection from potential competitors.

Scenario 59: Presentation at the Monopoly Convention

A natural monopoly is a market in which a single firm can satisfy the entire market demand more cheaply than two or more firms could. A natural monopoly is a distinct type of monopoly that may arise when there are extremely high fixed costs of distribution, such as exist when large-scale infrastructure is required to ensure supply. Examples of this type of infrastructure include cables and grids for electricity supply, pipelines for gas and water supply, and networks for rail and underground. These costs are effective barriers to exit and entry. Consider how much it would to start up a telephone company to provide telephone service to people in a certain area. Now compare that cost with the cost to an existing telephone company of providing the same service to those people. That explains why telephone companies, natural gas companies, electricity generation plants, and transportation systems are often monopolies.

Scenario 60: It's only a matter of time. Really?

The professor is incorrect on all counts. Here are the correct points:

1. The short run is a situation in which the firm has at least one factor of production.
2. The long run is a situation in which the firm can vary all its inputs, but its technology is fixed.
3. The very long run is a situation in which the firm can vary all its inputs, including its technology.

Scenario 61: Monopolist fails to maximize profits by deliberately not charging a higher price.

Total Electricity's pricing policy might be quite rational. By deliberately charging a price that is less than the profit-maximizing price, the company could be acting in a manner that would avoid it being regulated or even nationalized, that is, being taken over by the government. Also, the company could be creating a "caring company" image that could be beneficial in terms of customer loyalty.

Scenario 62: Can't Miss the Quiz

Answers

1. The demand curve for a firm in pure competition is horizontal.
2. False. It is minimizing its losses and should continue to operate.
3. d
4. A profit-seeking monopolist is not interested in charging the highest possible price for its product. It is interested in maximizing its profits and will therefore operate at a price where marginal revenue equals marginal cost.
5. Price discrimination is the practice of selling a product in different markets at different prices for reasons unrelated to cost.

Scenario 63: Who are they?

On the basis of the information provided, the economists pictured are Joan Robinson and Edward Chamberlin.

Scenario 64: Name that Market Structure

The features described indicate that the market structure is monopolistic competition.

Scenario 65: Different strokes for different taxis

Cross-Town Taxi must differentiate its product and publicize its differences from its competitors. It can do this by emphasizing its experience in the business, the quality of its services, the reliability of its services, and so on. These measures could set Cross-Town Taxi apart from its competitors.

Scenario 66: Advertising to the Rescue. We Love Chocolate

Hershey's customers must have been wary about the health risks involved in eating Hershey's candies. Some may even have switched to some of Hershey's competitors. An information advertising campaign aimed at educating and convincing customers of the safety of Hershey's candies could help to rectify the situation and regain many of the lost customers.

Scenario 67: Oligopoly—No General Theory Here

It is difficult to construct a general theory of oligopoly because behaviour in oligopoly markets depends so much on reactions from other firms. For example, if one firm raises its price, how will the others react? Several possibilities exist. We can make several different assumptions about the reactions of competitors. That explains why there are so many models of oligopoly.

Scenario 68: Internet Blames Hikes in the Price of Houses on Government Measures to Promote Competition

This seems to be a classic case of the post hoc, ergo propter hoc fallacy—the erroneous conclusion that one event causes another simply because it precedes the other. In this case, the conclusion on the Internet is that the increase in houses is due to the government's policy of preventing monopoly simply because the increase is the prices of houses follows the government's policy. Better explanations for the increase in the prices of houses are factors such

Scenario 69: A Kink in the Demand Curve? Oops! How Can This Be? Look at the Assumptions

A kink in the demand curve results from the assumptions that: (1) a price increase will not be matched by competitors and (2), a price reduction will be matched. The implication of a kinked demand curve is that a relatively small change in cost will not affect the price-quantity relationship that maximizes profits. This is illustrated by the following graph.

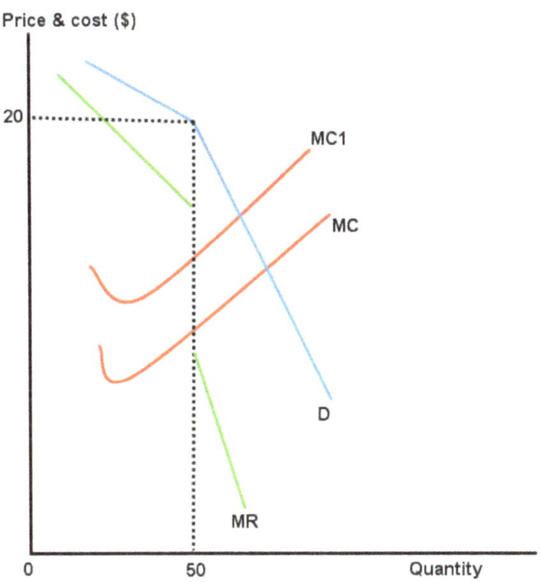

At a marginal cost of MC, the profit-maximizing price is \$20, and the quantity is 50. An increase in marginal cost to MC1 leaves the profit-maximizing price and quantity unchanged.

Scenario 70: Perplexing Questions about the Kink. Study Group to the Rescue

The professor would likely say that the originators of the kinked demand curve explained *how* a kink occurs in the demand curve, but they did not explain where the kink occurs. Also, they did not tell us how the price is determined in the first place. He would probably say that these are shortcomings of the model.

Scenario 71: Causes of Price Rigidity in Oligopoly Markets

The model of the kinked demand curve provides a reason for price rigidity in oligopoly markets; but that is not the only reason. Another reason is long-term contracts. If a firm has a long-term contract with a supplier to provide a certain good or service at a negotiated price, a small increase in price mat not affect the terms of the contract. Yet another reason for price rigidity is small menu costs. An example is changing the price tags on items in a supermarket. If a small change in cost occurs, it may be cheaper to leave the prices unchanged than to incur the cost of changing the prices.

Scenario 72: A Class Project—Cost-plus Pricing

Mark-up pricing, also known as cost-plus pricing, is a pricing strategy in which firms determine price by adding a certain percentage markup on cost. This pricing system has advantages and disadvantages. The advantage of this method of pricing is that it is easy to calculate and easy to understand. However, it has some disadvantages. If the firm is trying to maximize its profits, how does it know that a markup of 25% rather than a markup of 20% or 30% will equate marginal revenue and marginal cost? Second, the cost-plus is practical only if the firm knows exactly how much it can sell at various prices. If it puts its markup at 25%, it may find that it can sell only 70% of its output at that price. It may then be forced to lower its markup.

Scenario 73: Take Advantage of Cheap Labour Abroad

WebPro can take advantage of the relatively cheap labour in India by having its webpages designed there and then "exporting" them to Canada via the internet. By so doing, WebPro would significantly reduce cost and thus increase its profits.

Scenario 74: Tariffs? A Great Way for a Country to earn Income

Simply put, a tariff is a tax on foreign goods. The benefits of free trade are well known, yet the reality is that we live in a world of tariffs. Tariffs may be one way for a country to raise its income, but tariffs have some disadvantages. First, they interfere with free trade and prevent trading countries from benefiting from the free flow of goods. Second, they increase domestic prices which often place a burden on low and middle-income people. Third, tariffs lead to retaliation which often leads to a fall in income and an increase in unemployment in exporting industries. Finally, the imposition of tariffs often protects inefficiency as it enables the protected industry to operate with little pressure to be competitive.

Scenario 75: Currency Tied to Oil?

The external value of the Oilando currency is determined by demand and supply. When the price of oil rises, it will have little or no impact on the quantity of Oilando oil demanded by Undercan. Undercan will therefore require more Oilando dollars to pay for oil. This increase in demand for Oilando dollars, other things being equal, will increase the value of the Oilando dollar in terms of Undercan dollars. This explains the close relationship between the price of oil and the value of the Oilando currency.

Scenario 76: How Much Does It Cost? Can I Afford It? It's British. That Depends on the Exchange Rate

1. The price of the car is £35,000. With the exchange rate being £1 = $1.95, the price of the car in dollars would be:

35,000 × 1.95 = $68,250

Since David wants to spend no more than $65,000 for the car, he cannot afford to buy it.

2. In order for him to be able to afford the car, £35,000 would have to be equal to $65,000. This means that £1 would have to be equal to:

65,000 ÷ 35,000 = $1.86

The exchange rate would have to fall from £1 = $1.95 to £1 = $1.86

Scenario 77: To Flex or Not to Flex: Advantages and Disadvantages of Flexible Exchange Rates

A flexible exchange rate system is one in which the exchange rate is determined by the market forces of demand and supply. This exchange rate regime has advantages and disadvantages as indicated in the following table.

Advantages and Disadvantages of a Flexible Exchange Rate System

Advantages	Disadvantages
No direct intervention is necessary to achieve equilibrium in the foreign exchange market. The exchange rate adjusts automatically to changes in demand and supply and thus maintains equilibrium. There is therefore no need to maintain foreign reserves in order to peg the exchange rate. A flexible exchange rate frees monetary policy so that it can be used to stabilize the economy. A flexible exchange rate system helps to insulate a country against foreign inflationary pressures. Suppose there is inflation in country B while country A is experiencing relative price stability. Exports from country A to country B will increase as residents of country B switch to relatively cheaper goods from country A. At the same time, imports into country A from country B will fall as residents of country A reduce the quantity of relatively expensive goods demanded from country B. The resulting increase in demand for goods from country A will tend to increase prices in country A. The exchange rate will rise and thus prevent prices in country A from rising. The inflation in country B does not spill over into country A.	The uncertainty associated with flexible exchange rates discourages the flow of international trade. It is important for international traders to know what they will pay for their imports of goods and services that they will receive for their exports of goods and services. Trade cannot be expected to flourish in an environment of uncertainty and insecurity. Flexible exchange rates may affect a country adversely. For example, an appreciation of the value of country A's currency means that foreign goods become relatively less expensive to residents of country A. Lower-priced imports will then compete with goods produced in country A, and consumers may purchase foreign goods instead of goods produced in country A. This, in turn, may lead to reductions in income and increases in unemployment in country A.

Test 1

PART 1: DEFINITIONS (10 MARKS)

1. (a) Social science: Social science is any discipline that studies human behaviour. Examples of social science are economics, sociology, political science, and psychology

(b) Positive statement: A positive statement is a statement about facts and can be verified empirically. An example of a positive statement is: *six hundred students enrolled in economics this semester.*

(c) Rent: Rent is the income earned from land. If you hire out your private lake on the weekends, the income thus earned is rent.

(d) Production possibility (p-p) schedule: A p-p schedule is a table that shows the various combinations of goods and services that an economy can produce if it uses all its resources and if technology is constant. The following is an example of a p-p schedule where Qa is the quantity of A and Qb is the quantity of B that the economy can produce.

Qa	Qb
0	6
1	4
2	2
3	0

(e) Product market: The product market, also called the *goods and services market*, is the market in which goods and services are exchanged. The market where one buys shoes is an example of a product market.

2b	3d	4d	5b	6d
7b	8c	9d	10b	11d
12c	13c	14c	15b	16a
17b	18c	19b	20a	21c

PART 3: PROBLEMS AND EXERCISES (5 MARKS)

22. Production-Possibility Curves

Legend: ________ = original, ----------- = new

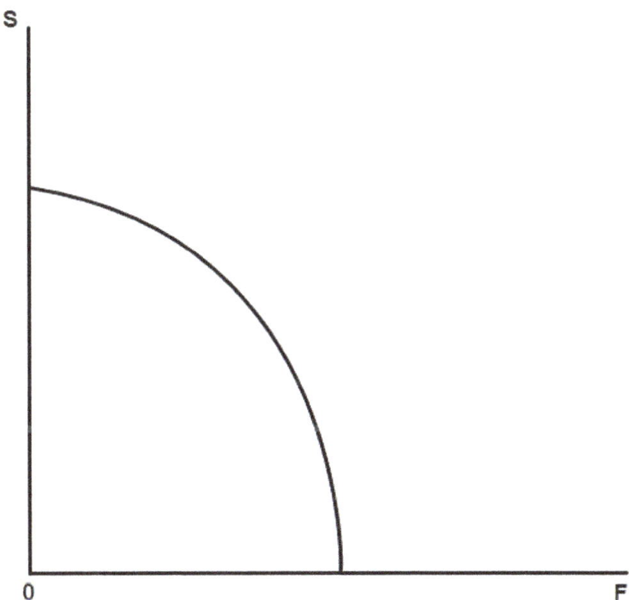

(a) A change in the prices of furniture and smartphones does not affect the economy's ability to produce these items; therefore the curve does not shift.

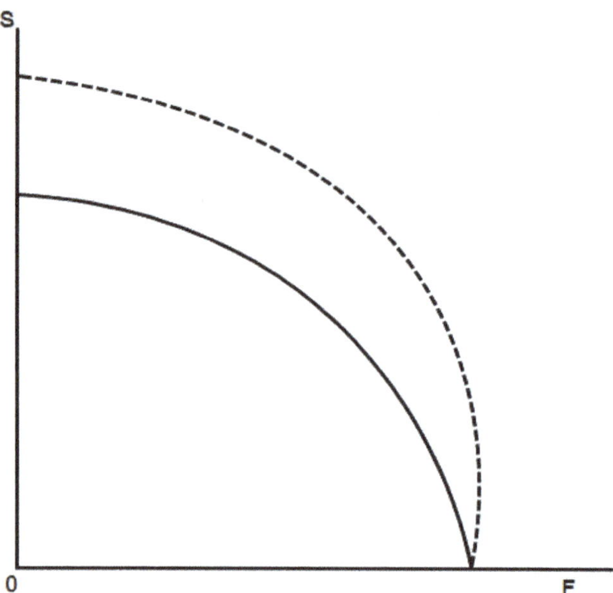

(b) This results in a non-parallel shift of the P-P curve as shown.

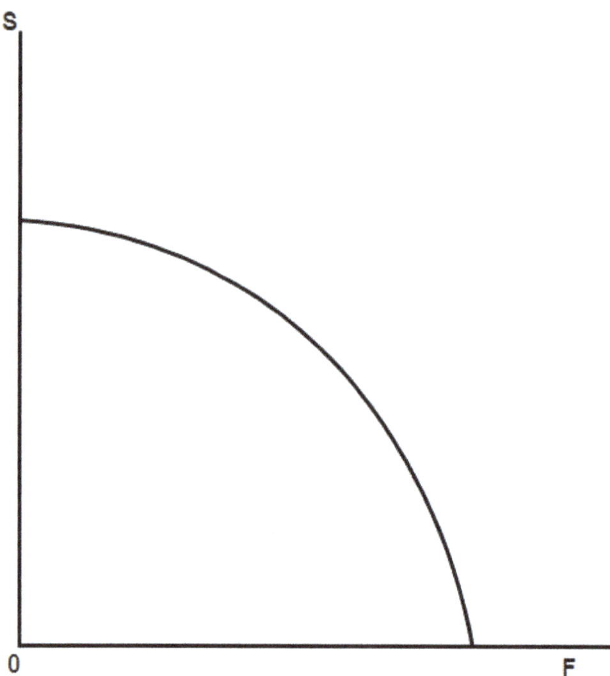

(c) The economy's productive capacity is not affected; therefore the P-P curve does not shift.

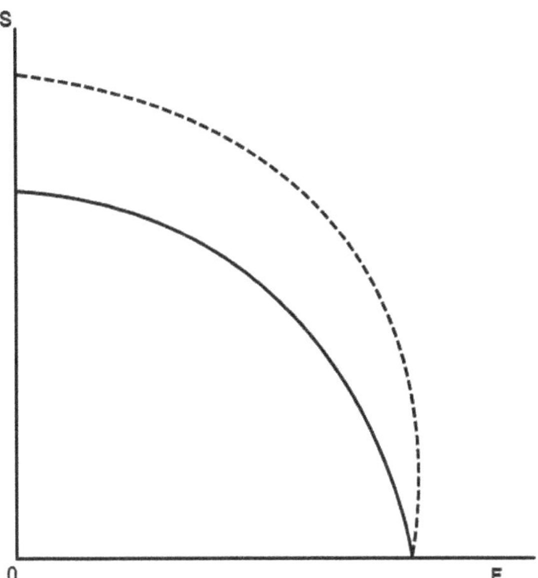

(d) The ability to produce smart phones has increased but there is no change in the ability to produce furniture. There is a non-parallel shift as shown.

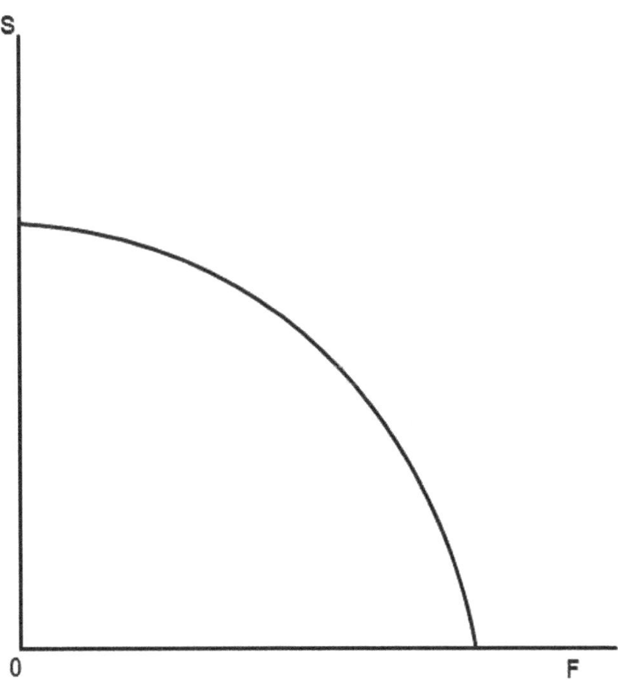

(e) There is no change in the economy's capacity to produce either smart phones or furniture; therefore the P-P curve does not shift.

PART 4: ESSAY QUESTION (5 MARKS)

23. (a) An economic model is a simplification of a real economy or some aspect of it—an abstraction from reality—and it consists only of the factors that appear to pertain most to what is being studied. Details that do not pertain directly to the question or problem being studied are simply stripped away in the model.

(b) Economic models simplify economic reality. The real economy is extremely complex, much more so than is realized at first glance, and without models that reduce the complexities to manageable dimensions, economists (and those who study the economy) would not learn much about how a real economy functions. Through the construction and use of economic models, economists are able to get a much clearer understanding about economic processes and problems such as inflation, unemployment, economic growth, and business cycles.

Test 1A (Alternative)

PART 1: DEFINITIONS (10 MARKS)

1. (a) Real capital: Real capital is any manufactured item that can be used to produce goods and services. Buildings, roads, manufacturing plants (factories), equipment, and tools are examples of real capital. Money is usually classified as financial capital.

(b) Flow: A flow (or a flow variable) is a measure of the change during a period of time. An example of a flow is a salary of $700 per week.

(c) Relative scarcity: Relative scarcity (also referred to as economic scarcity) refers to situations in which there are not enough resources to produce all the goods and services that would be necessary to satisfy all human wants.

(d) Endogenous variable: An endogenous variable is a variable whose value is determined within the model. For example, if we say that the quantity of tablets that people will buy depends on the price of tablets, then price would be an endogenous variable.

(e) Positive statement: A positive statement is an expression of how something is as opposed to how it ought to be. It is objective and based on facts. The following is an example of a positive statement: *Those who do a great deal of reading tend to get better grades in economics.*

PART 2: MULTIPLE-CHOICE QUESTIONS (20 MARKS)

2d	3c	4b	5d	6c
7b	8c	9d	10a	11b
12c	13d	14d	15b	16d
17a	18d	9d	20a	21d

22. Production-Possibility Curve

Legend: _________ = original; ----------- = new

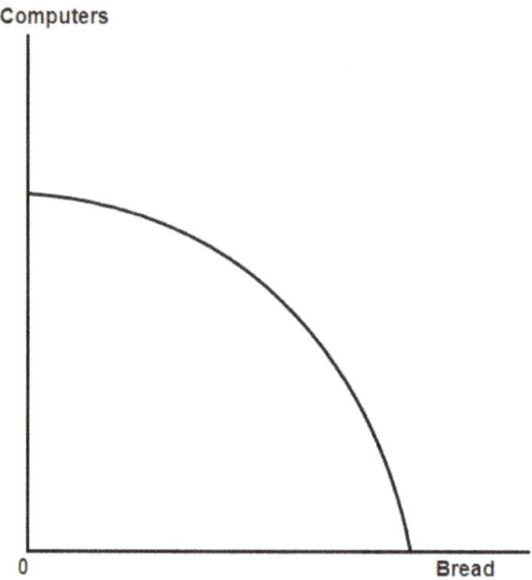

a. The P-P curve remains the same but the actual production combination would change.

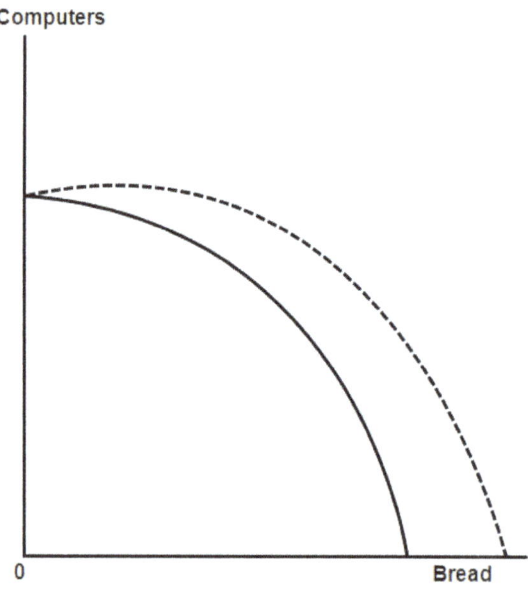

b. The economy's ability to produce bread increases but its ability to produce computers is not affected. This results in a non-parallel shift in the P-P curve as shown.

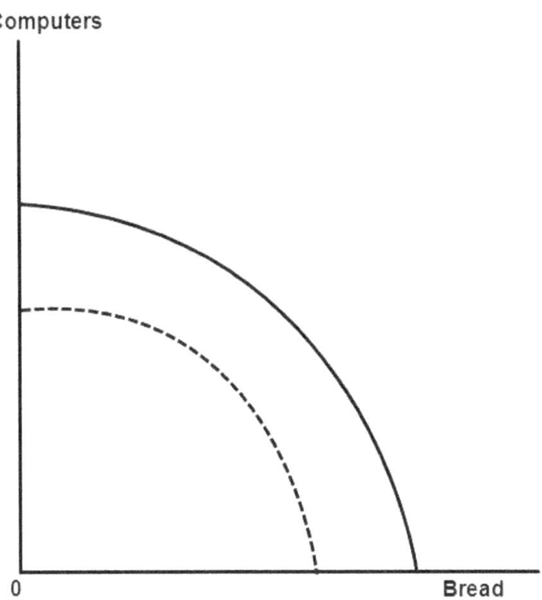

c. The economy suffers a loss of resources; therefore, the P-P curve shifts to the left as shown.

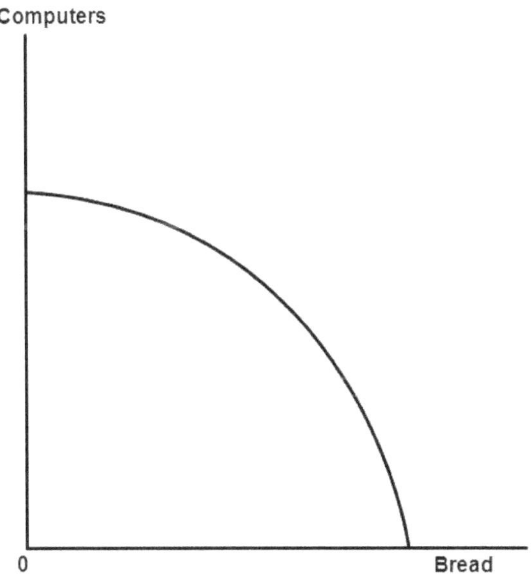

d. The P-P curve does not shift because the economy's productive capacity is not affected.

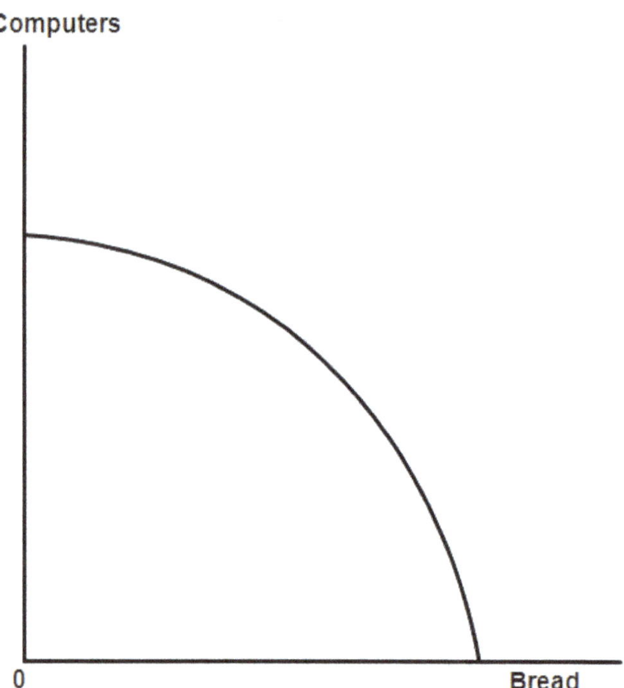

(e) There is no change in the P-P curve because the economy's ability to produce computers and bread is not affected.

PART 4: ESSAY QUESTION (5 MARKS)

23. (a) An economic model is a hypothetical construct containing simplifying assumptions and hypotheses. Because the model is an abstraction from reality, it makes it easier to understand the relationships among economic variables. The model may be constructed using words, graphs, or mathematics.

(b) Economists construct models because it makes it easier for them to understand economic phenomena and processes, and thus helps them to get a clearer grasp of how the economy actually functions. Without the help of economic models, it would be much more difficult to understand the complexities of the real economy.

(c) One can determine the goodness of a model by how well it explains economic reality. The whole purpose of an economic model is to help us to explain some aspect of economic reality and to make predictions about economic outcomes. An economic model that does this well is a good model. If the model fails to explain economic reality, then it cannot be considered a good model.

Test 2

PART 1. DEFINITIONS

1 a. A supply curve is a graph that shows the direct relation between price and quantity offered for sale.

b. Price elasticity of demand is a measure of the degree to which quantity demanded responds to a change in price.

c. A budget line is a line on a graph that shows all combinations of goods that the consumer can buy for the same amount of money.

d. The marginal product of labour is the extra output produced by using an additional unit of labour.

e. Variable cost is cost that varies with the volume of output. Examples of variable costs are wages and the cost of raw material.

PART 2. MULTIPLE-CHOICE (20 MARKS)

2a	3c	4c	5a	6b
7c	8b	9c	10c	11a
12b	13c	14b	15a	16b
17c	18b	19c	20a	21a

PART 3. PROBLEMS AND EXERCISES (5 MARKS)

22. Effect on equilibrium price and equilibrium quantity.

________ = Original; ----------- = New

a. A decrease in enrolment would decrease the demand for reading lamps. As shown in the following diagram, the demand curve shifts from D to D0. This causes the equilibrium price to fall from P to P0 and the equilibrium quantity to fall from Q to Q0.

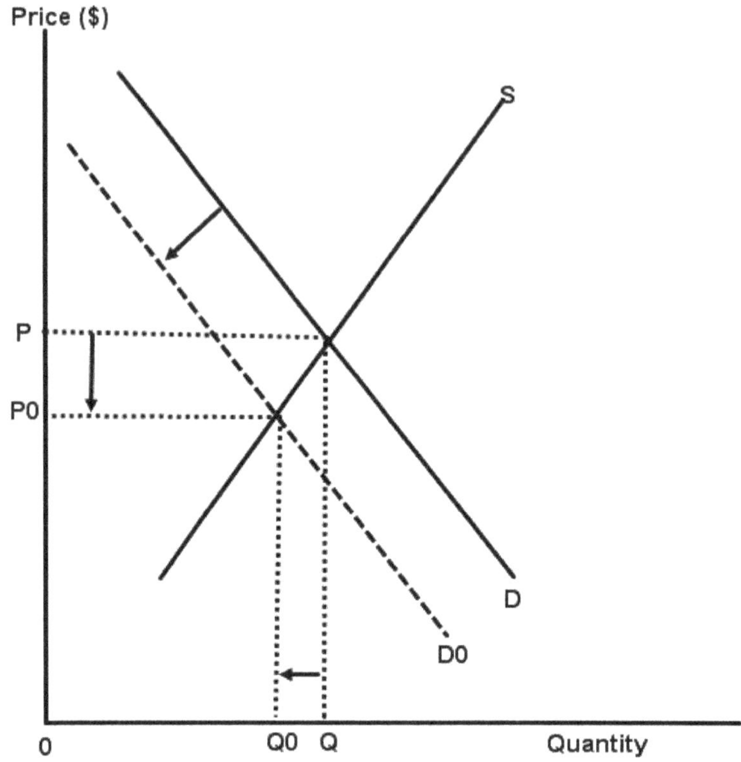

b. The announcement will likely increase the demand for reading lamps as shown below.

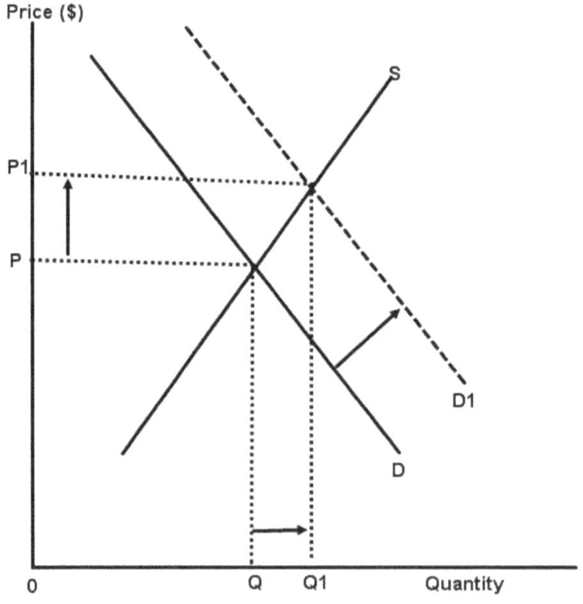

The price will rise from P to P1, and the quantity will also rise from Q to Q1.

c. A decrease in cost will increase the supply as shown in the following graph. The equilibrium price will fall, and the equilibrium quantity will increase.

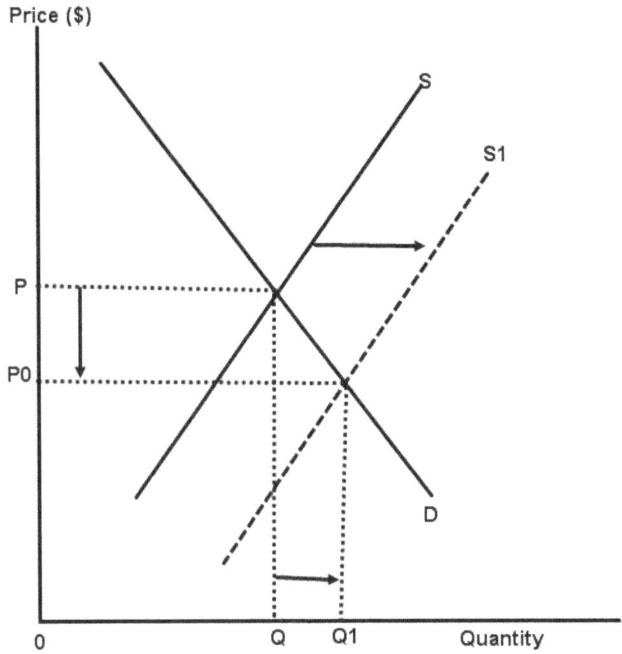

d. This better technology will increase the supply of reading lamps, which will lower the equilibrium price and increase the equilibrium quantity as shown in the graph below.

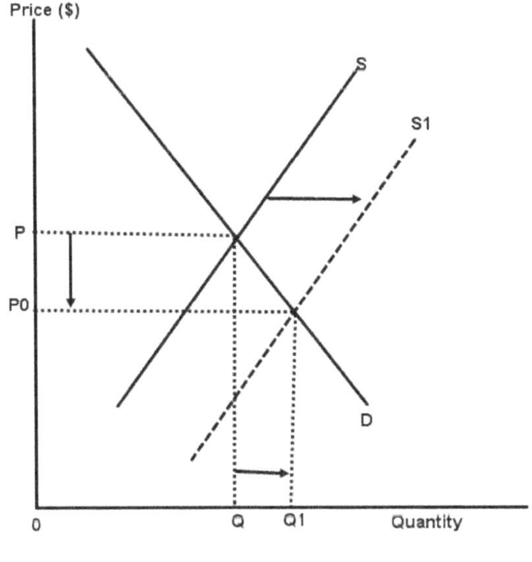

e. An increase in consumers' income will increase the demand for reading lamps. As shown in the following diagram, this will increase equilibrium price and equilibrium quantity.

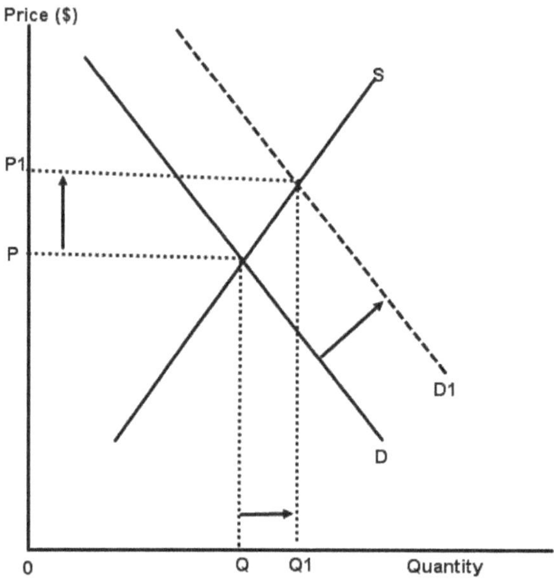

PART 4. ESSAY QUESTION (5 MARKS)

The average fixed cost (AFC) curve declines continuously because it is TFC/Q. Total fixed cost (the numerator) is constant, so as Q (the denominator) increases, the fraction smaller and smaller. The total fixed cost is spread over an increasing quantity of output.

Test 2A

PART 1. DEFINITION

1. a. A demand schedule is a table that shows the various quantities of an item that people will buy at various prices. An example follows.

Price ($)	Quantity demanded
6	100
5	110
4	120
3	130

b. The equilibrium quantity is the quantity bought and sold at the equilibrium price.

c. An inferior good is a good such that as income rises, people buy less of it. An example of an inferior good is used tires.

d. Income elasticity of demand is a measure of the degree to which demand changes as a result of a change in income.

e. A cost function is an equation that expresses a relation between cost and output. An example of a cost function is: $C = f(Q)$ where C is cost and Q is output.

PART 2. MULTIPLE-CHOICE (20 MARKS)

2d	3d	4b	5d	6d
7c	8b	9d	10d	11c
12c	13b	14a	15b	16a
17d	18c	19c	20d	21a

PART 3. PROBLEMS AND EXERCISES (5 MARKS)

22. Effect on equilibrium price and equilibrium quantity.

a. In this case, there will be an increase in demand, so equilibrium price and quantity will rise as shown in the diagram below.

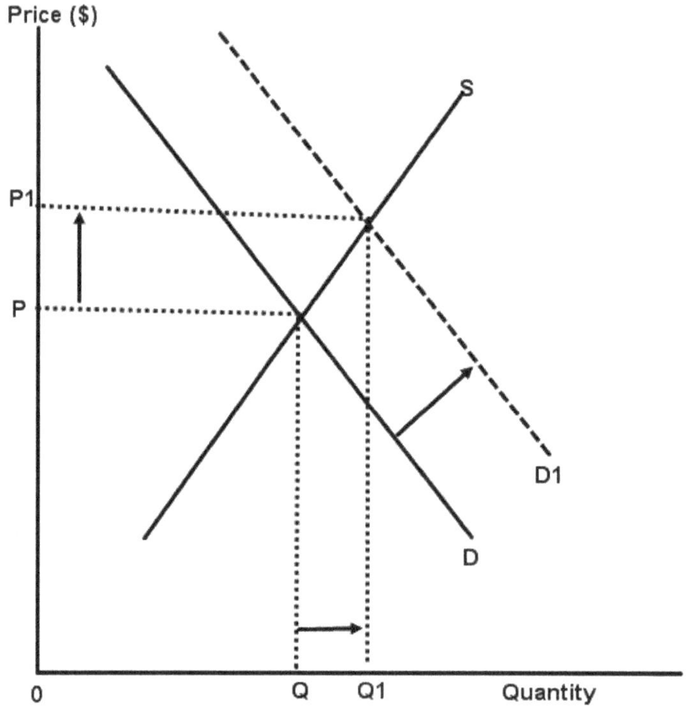

b. Since students use pencil cases, the demand for pencil cases will increase, thus rising the equilibrium price and the equilibrium quantity.

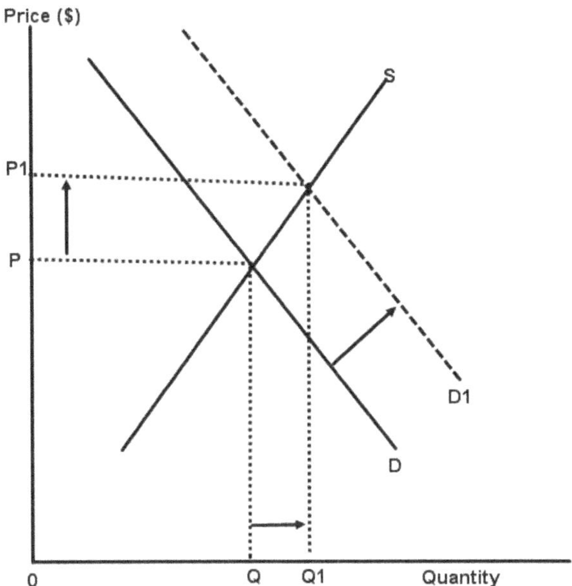

c. This will increase the supply of pencil cases. The equilibrium price will fall and the equilibrium quantity will increase as shown in the diagram below.

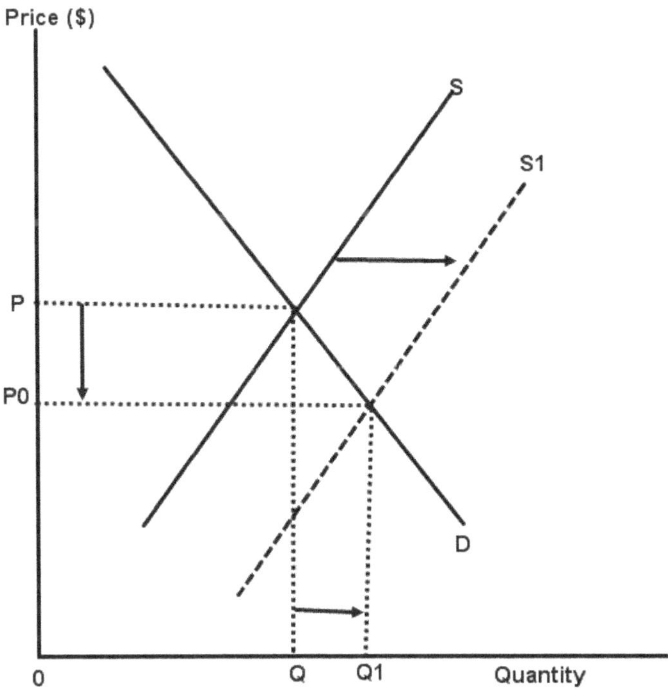

d. This will reduce the supply. The equilibrium price will rise and the equilibrium quantity will fall as shown in the following diagram.

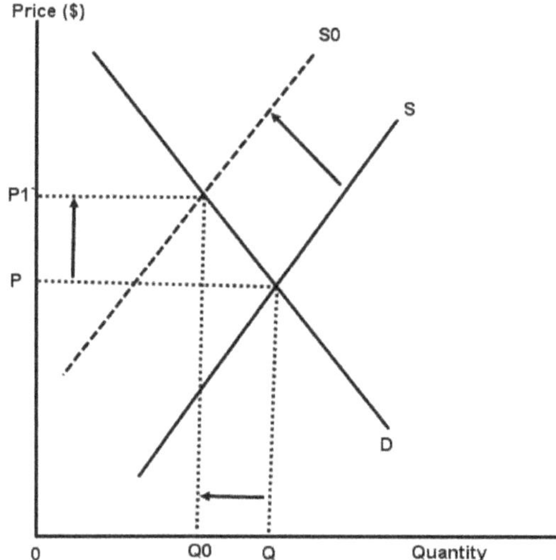

e. A decrease in the prices of pens and pencils will cause people to buy more pens and pencils, thus increasing the demand for pencil cases. As shown in the diagram below, the equilibrium price will rise and the equilibrium quantity will also rise.

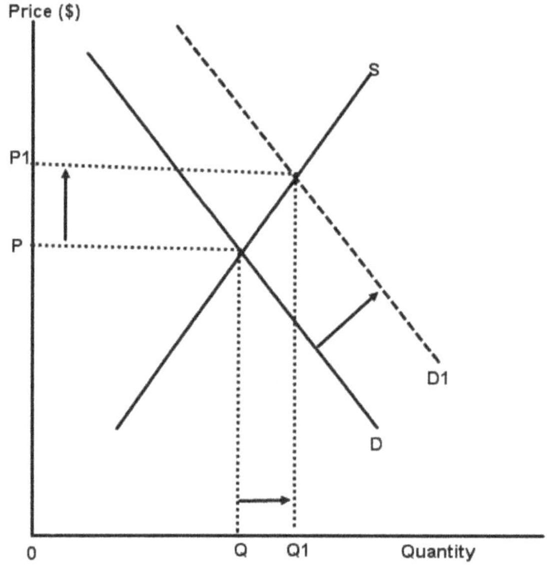

PART 4. ESSAY QUESTIONS (5 MARKS)

23. Reasons for Increasing and Decreasing Returns to Scale

One reason for increasing returns to scale is specialization. A large-scale operation may be able to take advantage of specialization which may not be practical in a smaller scale operation. A second reason for increasing returns to scale is quantity discounts. A large-scale operation may be able to purchase inputs at a lower cost than can a smaller operation. Finally, dimensional factors may cause increasing returns to scale. For example, a storage space that is 4 m × 4 m × 4 m can hold 64 cubic meters of material. Doubling the dimensions will more than double the storage capacity.

It is generally agreed that the main reason for decreasing returns to scale or increasing costs is inefficiency in management. As the scale of operation expands, it becomes increasingly difficult to manage the operation.

Test 3

PART 1. DEFINITIONS (10 MARKS)

1.

a. Pure competition is a market structure consisting of a large number of firms selling homogeneous products. There is freedom of entry and exit into and from this industry, and each firm is a price-taker.

b. Marginal revenue is the extra revenue obtained from selling an additional unit of output.

c. Barriers to entry are restrictions that prevent firms from entering a market.

d. Duopoly is a market structure in which there are only two firms.

e. Product differentiation is the condition that exists when firms distinguish their products from those of their competitors.

PART 2. MULTIPLE CHOICE (20 MARKS)

2c	3d	4b	5d	6b
7c	8a	9d	10d	11a
12d	13a	14d	15b	16a
17d	18b	19d	20a	21c

PART 3. PROBLEMS AND EXERCISES (5 MARKS)

22.

a. This firm should produce 60 units of output to maximize its profits.

b. The firm should a price of $12.

c. The maximum profit the firm can make is $180.

d. At a price of $9, the total revenue will be $675.

e. At $12, the total revenue will be $600, so total revenue will fall.

23. The firm may have other objectives than to maximize profits. For example, it may want to achieve a satisfactory level of profits. The firm can be in equilibrium even if it's not making a profit. In the short run, the firm will be in equilibrium if marginal revenue equals marginal cost. This can occur when the price is above average variable cost and below average total cost. In this case, the firm will be minimizing its losses. In the long run, a firm in pure competition will be in equilibrium when its marginal revenue is equal to its marginal cost, and its profit will be zero.

Test 3A (Alternative)

PART 1. DEFINITIONS (10 MARKS)

1. a. A price-taker is a firm that has no control over the price of its product. A firm in pure competition is an example of a price-taker.

b. Pareto optimality is the condition that exists when it is impossible to make someone else better off without making someone else worse off.

c. Price discrimination is the practice of selling a product in different markets at different prices for reasons not associated with cost.

d. Collusion is the act of getting together to control price and output in particular markets.

e. Workable competition is the condition that exists when competition is sufficient to ensure that market power is not excessive.

PART 2. MULTIPLE-CHOICE (20 MARKS)

2d	3b	4b	5d	6c
7d	8b	9b	10a	11d
12b	13d	14a	15c	16b
17b	18b	19d	20d	21c

PART 3. PROBLEMS AND EXERCISES

22. a. The firm should produce 60 units of output where MR=MC.

b. The firm should charge a price of $14.

c. The firm should not adjust its price or output.

PART 4. ESSAY (5 MARKS)

23. A cartel is a formal agreement among independent firms to act in concert to control price and output in a particular industry. A real-world example of a cartel is the Organization of the Petroleum Exporting Countries (OPEC). Some of the problems faced by cartels include:

(i) the unwillingness of cartel members to sacrifice their decision-making powers to a central body;

(ii) the strong temptation for members to cheat and produce more than the prescribed quantity;

(iii) the cartel may be threatened by the entry of new firms into the market.

www.ingramcontent.com/pod-product-compliance
Lightning Source LLC
Chambersburg PA
CBHW080832160726
47999CB00009B/2862